"*The Stonewall Generation* is a critical additi~~on~~ ~~~~ ~~~~ ~~~~ ~~~~ ~~his~~ tory and sociology. Generous, th ~~~~ ~~~~ ~~~~ brought on many memories. ~~~~ how glad I am I came out and g

   —Kate Clinton, comedia~~n~~ ~~~~ ~~~~ ~~~~ ~~~~ ~~Name~~
    Started and *I Told You S*~~o~~

"*The Stonewall Generation* is a gem of a book, with interviews that illuminate different aspects of LGBTQ life in the United States and how aging intersects with identity, activism, and sex. Jane Fleishman's thoughtful commentary and historical notes make it perfect for people who may be less familiar with LGBTQ history, and I think everyone will find something surprising or inspiring in these pages."

   —Tim Johnston, Senior Director of National Projects
    at SAGE, author of *Welcoming LGBT Residents:*
    A Practical Guide for Senior Living Staff

"*The Stonewall Generation* offers a compelling intervention to two facets of anti-LGBTQ oppression that have been ignored for too long: the erasure of our elders and the dispossession of our history. These oral histories offer candor, charisma, and caution to illuminate hidden pasts and inform our movement's future. A must read."

   —Alok Vaid-Menon, trans writer and performance artist,
    author of *Beyond the Gender Binary*

"*The Stonewall Generation* is a wonderful read, full of the vibrant and distinct life experiences of these LGBT older adults, and Jane Fleishman anchors them all with the question 'where were you on June 28, 1969?' This is living history—from a few who were in the Stonewall bar that evening to those who weren't even aware of it. Each voice tells a unique story that blends together with the others and offers us the history of our oppression and the resiliency of our community. What better way to honor and appreciate this generation of LGBT older adults?"

   —Lisa Krinsky, Director of the LGBT Aging Project,
    The Fenway Institute

"*The Stonewall Generation* is a historical account of June 28, 1969, and the LGBTQ activists whose lives were changed by that event, but it is much more than that. It is the powerful, intensely personal narrative of LGBTQ elders who tell their life stories in their own words. Jane Fleishman skillfully pieces together her interviews so that the speakers come to life for us. We learn about their coming out process, how and why they became activists, how Stonewall changed them, what their sexuality was like in their youth, and what it is for them now, as elders. This is a stunning book that gives voice and visibility to people who have been largely ignored by our society. It's time to listen to them."

> —Joan Price, advocate for ageless sexuality, author of the award-winning *Naked at Our Age: Talking Out Loud About Senior Sex* and *Sex After Grief: Navigating Your Sexuality After Losing Your Beloved*

"Jane Fleishman's *The Stonewall Generation* captures the thoughts, voices, and experiences of older folks across the LGBTQIAA+ spectrum in a way that both humanizes and glorifies them, honoring their lives and their legacies, who they are, and how they fought for the freedoms we might not otherwise have today. In particular, Fleishman is adept at candidly discussing elder LGBTQIAA+ *sex*, not just *sexual identity*. Too often, what we identify as is given primacy, and what we do in the bedroom is glossed over—particularly when discussing the lives of elders. This creates different, but no less destructive silences. *The Stonewall Generation* fills these gaps in our collective knowledge with the joyful, tearful, and always heartfelt reminiscences of a group of brave—and unflappable—elders."

> —Hugh Ryan, author of *When Brooklyn Was Queer*

"Jane Fleishman's intimate and uncensored personal histories provide unique accounts of LGBTQ life in the sixties and seventies. The dynamic personal reflections expand understanding and empathy and are a welcome and much-needed resource."

> —Melanie Davis, PhD, Co-President, Sexuality and Aging Consortium at Widener University

"A dazzling volume that shows how to value the voices of LGBT elders, *The Stonewall Generation* connects the struggles of the LGBT liberation generation directly to the present day. By featuring the stories of those who were at Stonewall and the many who were not, Jane Fleishman places race, class, and trans diversity back at the heart of their legacy, where they belong. Treating its contributors not as living history, but as living leaders with great wisdom on sex, activism, and flourishing in the face of oppression, the book's interviews and commentary are more important than ever. *The Stonewall Generation* is essential reading for educators, allies, and everyone in queer and trans communities, who deserve a rich and storied relationship to their elders."

> —Jules Gill-Peterson, Associate Professor of English, University of Pittsburgh, and author of *Histories of the Transgender Child*

"*The Stonewall Generation* slowly became a mirror as I read it, in which I could reflect on my own unique story amidst the stories of others. As an unabashedly candid oral history, it summoned me to both unexpected insights and tears flowing in solidarity and witness. A member of the Stonewall generation myself—part of the 30,000 strong candle-light march on the night of Harvey Milk's murder in San Francisco—I felt as if I knew each person in this book, even though I have never met them. The storytellers' ways of talking about age, discovering themselves, and sexuality, strengthened my confidence in the possibility of a more hopeful future for all of us."

> —Rev. Dr. Mark Belletini, author of *Nothing Gold Can Stay* and *Sonata for Voice and Silence*

The Stonewall Generation

LGBTQ ELDERS ON SEX, ACTIVISM, AND AGING

Jane Fleishman

Skinner House Books
Boston

www.skinnerhouse.org

Printed in the United States

Cover design by Kathryn Sky-Peck
Text design by Jeff Miller

print ISBN: 978-1-55896-853-0
eBook ISBN: 978-1-55896-854-7

5 4
24 23

Library of Congress Cataloging-in-Publication Data
Names: Fleishman, Jane, 1954– author.
Title: The Stonewall generation : LGBTQ elders on sex, activism, and
    aging / [edited by] Jane Fleishman.
Description: Boston : Skinner House Books, [2020] | Includes
    bibliographical references and index. | Summary: "Sexuality researcher
    Jane Fleishman shares the stories of nine fearless elders in the LGBTQ
    community who came of age around the time of Stonewall. In candid
    interviews, they lay bare their struggles, their strengths, their activism,
    and their sexual liberation in the context of the political movements of
    the 1960s and 1970s and today"—Provided by publisher.
Identifiers: LCCN 2020001469 (print) | LCCN 2020001470 (ebook) |
    ISBN 9781558968530 (paperback) | ISBN 9781558968547 (ebook)
Subjects: LCSH: Older sexual minorities. | Sexual minority community—
    United States—History.
Classification: LCC HQ76.27.O44 S76 2020 (print) | LCC HQ76.27.O44
    (ebook) | DDC 306.76084/6—dc23
LC record available at https://lccn.loc.gov/2020001469
LC ebook record available at https://lccn.loc.gov/2020001470

This book is dedicated to my parents,
Enid and Norman,
my children, Ezra and Rosie,
and my lover, Joan.

Each of you has given me the strength,
support, and love to carry on the fight
for sexual freedom and justice.

Contents

A Note on Language

During the Stonewall era, people in the LGBTQ community described themselves a bit differently than they do today. For instance, people who would today describe themselves as transgender, nonbinary, or genderqueer were much more likely to express their gender or sexual identity as drag queen or butch. These terms don't line up completely with today's terms for these identities because understandings have changed and meanings have shifted over the intervening years.

Many of the terms used today by people in the LGBTQ community may have been understood in different ways during the time of Stonewall. I myself have been surprised at some of the ways people described themselves. Some of the people I interviewed might have identified themselves differently if that language had been available to them. And they might refer to their own identities in ways that contemporary readers might find surprising and outdated, but I have chosen to honor their right to name themselves for themselves and not second-guess them.

Some of the language you'll read in the interviews may not feel comfortable to you. Language is changing so quickly that we cannot even imagine what language will be like in the future. During the early days of the modern LGBTQ liberation movement, the community and the movement were often referred to as a "gay community" and "gay rights movement." Reviewing how we spoke of our movement over the past five decades could be the subject of an entire book. Some of the people I interview in the book use the term "gay and lesbian community," which was in vogue until the 1980s until bisexual people fought for and won the right to be included on banners and marches as "GLB" or later "LGB" seeing the primacy of women in the movement. It wasn't until very recently that the term "LGBT" has been used to be more inclusive of transgender people. Lately, the term has been expandeed to LGBTQ signifying the reclamation of the term "queer," which some have traced back to the HIV/AIDS epidemic of the 1990s, when the group Queer Nation organized as a radical group to stop violence against the community. Shifts in language often occur inside the community earlier and take longer to percolate out into mainstream usage. As our movement has become more inclusive, I've been in conferences where the initials get even longer LGBTQIAAP+ (adding intersex, asexual, ally, pansexual, polyamorous, non-binary, plus horizons beyond). It's all about inclusion. Writing about these historical periods through a lens of our current understanding of the breadth of the spectrum of sexual and gender identity, I will refer to the community and the movement in inclusive terms that feel right at this moment, without using the word *queer*, which has been appropriated in a positive way by many in the LGBTQ+ community but is still considered offensive by many, particularly in the generation that the people I interviewed for this book belong to.

Foreword

There's an old joke about Woodstock that could just as easily apply to Stonewall. Basically, it says that if everyone who claims to have been there had really been there, the crowd size would be equal to the population of a not-so-small European country. Funny—and true. Why do so many of us who were alive and aware in 1969 feel like we were at Stonewall or Woodstock? Probably because both these events, which happened only two months apart, were such huge cultural milestones that they transcended a place or a date. They washed over us like a tsunami, changing the landscape of our lives forever. And although they were gatherings attended by relatively few, they changed everything for millions of people worldwide.

So it's logical that the first question Jane asks all her interviewees in *The Stonewall Generation* is "Where were

you on the night of June 28, 1969?" And this time everyone who's asked tells the truth, including us:

On June 28, 1969, Kate was sitting quietly in their car,
staring up at a moose who was standing in the middle of
the Trans-Canada Highway. She was going to San Francisco. Kate had missed 1967's Summer of Love and was
going in search of sloppy seconds. Surely, there would still
be hippies and hippie chicks lining the sidewalks of
Haight Ashbury. At the time, Kate was a hippie boy who
wanted to be a hippie chick: twenty-one years old, just out
of college, and about to start graduate school in the fall.
The only trans people Kate's age who were out of the closet
were those who wouldn't fit into a closet: those whose
gender expression was too boldly and proudly queer to
allow for any hiding away. These were the self-defined
queens and fairies and butch women who in those days
were consigned to marginalized lives on the streets. That
was the cost of being a gender outlaw in 1969. *Trans* wasn't
even a word yet—the phenomenon of transsexuality was
barely noticed by the mainstream media. Kate called them-
self a freak, but they didn't want the rest of the world calling them a freak too. Hippie boys could grow their hair
long and wear pretty headbands, bell bottoms, and flow-
ered shirts. Kate would have to make do with her delight
in that small piece of gender freedom for a while. Kate
wouldn't hear about Stonewall for another fifteen years.

Barbara was a teenager in Newport, Rhode Island,
deeply mourning the death of Judy Garland while

celebrating her first professional theater job as an apprentice with a local summer stock company. She doesn't recall hearing about Stonewall in any meaningful way until the following winter when she became friends with Paul, a twenty-something gay sound designer at her community theatre. He was ecstatic about the possibilities that the Stonewall Riots and gay liberation, as they were called at the time, would bring, and his enthusiasm was infectious. Interestingly enough, the thing Barbara and Paul were most passionate about being liberated from was marriage. They were convinced that gay people would be able to model a lifestyle that would convince straight people that marriage was outmoded and anti-liberation. (Ah well . . . win some, lose some.)

Gay Liberation, Women's Liberation, Black Liberation, Sexual Liberation. Liberation was the heart and soul of the years following June 28, 1969, for Barbara, as it was for so many others.

Like us, not all the people who share their stories in *The Stonewall Generation* were "in the room where it happened"—that is, on the front lines resisting the police. Many did not pick up the activist baton until several years later, yet their contribution is just as important to the history of the Stonewall phenomenon as if they'd been loaded into the police vans on June 28. Many of the people interviewed for this book were marginalized not only by the mainstream culture but also by folks within their already marginalized culture for various reasons: for being too effeminate, too butch, too kinky, too bisexual, or for being people of color, sex workers, or drag queens. Our biggest delight and immense gratitude for this book rests in the choice of people who were included. Because the vast majority of us were not at Stonewall (or Woodstock), we have tended to interpret the event through the narrow historic lens of the dominant culture. Until relatively recently, most people thought of Stonewall as a primarily white, middle class, gay male event. *The Stonewall Generation* strips away this whitewashed, classist, sexist, and sex-negative veneer.

We also celebrate the author's decision not to edit the voices of these elders. We all spoke a different language of liberation fifty years ago, particularly those of us in hyper-marginalized communities, and it's important for us to remember what our struggles and victories sounded like in the original language.

It is equally important for young people today to hear how differently things looked and sounded in 1969, while still being able to appreciate the common yearnings for love, identity, and human rights that they are still fighting for today. As the saying goes, "History doesn't repeat itself, but it often rhymes." Social change is never a straight line. What goes down comes around in a spiral—not circling back to the same spot, but with each revolution, reaching a point a bit further away from the center as we expand our awareness and ability to include and connect with others.

Most importantly, *The Stonewall Generation* is a love story. In the midst of all the fights for our rights over the past decades, we were then and are still fighting to be loved for who we are, and to be able to love whomever we choose in the way we choose.

Perhaps you picked up this book because you remember life before and after Stonewall. Maybe you even know one of the people interviewed. Or maybe you've only just heard about Stonewall from a teacher at your school and you'd like to learn more about it from someone who was there. Welcome to the Time Capsule of Love that is *The Stonewall Generation*. The brave, youthful activists who have become our LGBTQ+ elders will inspire you—whatever your age—with the spirit and perseverance to shape your own LGBTQ+ future.

—Kate Bornstein & Barbara Carrellas

Kate Bornstein is a nonbinary author, performance artist, and gender theorist. Their books include *Gender Outlaw: On Men, Women, and the Rest of Us* and *Hello Cruel World: 101 Alternatives to Suicide for Teens, Freaks, and Other Outlaws*.

Barbara Carrellas is the founder of Urban Tantra®, an approach to sacred sexuality that adapts and blends a wide variety of conscious sexuality practices from Tantra to BDSM. Her books include *Urban Tantra: Sacred Sex for the Twenty-First Century* and *Ecstasy is Necessary: A Practical Guide to Sex, Relationships and Oh, So Much More*.

Introduction

The generation of LGBTQ people who came of age around the time of the Stonewall Rebellion lived their young adulthoods in a turbulent time, a time of fear, a time of secrecy. And yet, in the midst of it all, the Stonewall generation has continued to fight for freedom, for rights, for love, and, yes, for sex. Delving into our history can help to remind us of the courageous, inventive, and inspiring paths that LGBTQ people have taken toward liberation against a backdrop of fear. In this time when we need hope, when a wide swath of LGBTQ and other marginalized people are fearful that hard-won civil and human rights are being expunged and trampled upon, this book and the stories of the Stonewall generation can provide hope for those of us who've lived these struggles. They remind us of what we've been through and how far we've come. This book can also be a useful tool for younger people who want to understand the historical context for their elders' lives. This book can inform all of us, whatever our age or how we identify.

Traveling across the country for two years conducting these interviews, I asked each person about their struggles, their strengths, their politics, their sexual liberation as LGBTQ people, and what sex means to them now. I chose each person intentionally because each one has spent a lifetime fighting for liberation: for the right to live, to love, to be free.

As a sexuality researcher, I am primarily interested in the sexualities of those who are often overlooked, particularly older adults in the LGBTQ community. LGBTQ elders have been treated mostly as problems. Gay men have been demonized as spreading HIV and AIDS, being promiscuous, and abusing children; lesbians have been stereotyped as living grim and sexless lives; bisexual people have been accused of spreading AIDS to straight people and rendered invisible inside and outside their own communities; transgender and genderqueer people have been misunderstood completely. And most mainstream academic research on older adults leaves out LGBTQ elders altogether. In addition to being a researcher, I'm also an activist, and I've been interested in the impact early LGBTQ and other political struggles have had on these individuals' relationship histories, their sexual and gender identities, and their sexual lives today. I've wanted to write this book from the first day I started a statistical research project in 2013 on LGBTQ elders and the factors that enhance and impede their sexual satisfaction—factors like internalized homophobia, resilience, communication, and relationships. After completing that research, I wanted to look behind the statistics.

The invisibility of this group of elders is evident. These are baby boomers who have been part of the largest population bulge in U.S. history (except for millennials, who are now edging them out). When the AARP magazine arrives in my mailbox, why aren't there any stories about the achievements, struggles, love lives, setbacks, comebacks, and complexities of the lives of elders in the LGBTQ community? Why haven't we seen any stories illustrating the multiplicity of relationship types in the gay male community since the HIV/AIDS pandemic of the 1980s? Or the impacts of biphobia on bisexual members of the LGBTQ community? What about the experiences multiply marginalized LGBTQ elders of color face? Or the misconceptions about elder kinksters in the leather community? What about aging sex workers? What about aging drag queens, gender benders, members of the transgender community, and anyone whose gender exists outside the gender binary? What about the internalization of oppression so often holding individuals in the LGBTQ community back from full sexual expression? Or the oppression from within the LGBTQ community toward marginalized members who don't fit in with publicly held notions and stereotypes of sexual or gender minorities? I saw the need to answer these and so many other questions.

And I had so many more personal questions for the people I wanted to interview, questions they bravely and candidly answered. For many, it was extremely important to declare their sexual orientation or gender identity. (For many today, it's more important to stay flexible and fluid.) I wanted to ask my group of LGBTQ elders about that. What was their coming out like? What helped and hindered their process? What was sex like? What impact did Stonewall and other political movements have on their life? What lessons did they learn along the way?

I was particularly interested in questions of how their struggles as lesbian, gay, bi, or trans people might be exacerbated by factors of race, class, geography, and age. I wanted to find out how the community these individuals came out in received them. Were they the "right" kind of lesbians or gay men? Were they scrutinized more critically because they came out as bi? Was there insidious racism or classism keeping them down just when they thought they'd finally come home? Were they called names or looked down upon for choosing to be paid for sex in money or drugs, for being fat, for kinky sexual practices? Were their political credentials dissected when they wore the "wrong" kinds of clothes or lived in the "wrong" kinds of places? What political movements made an impact on them? How did their sexual lives as younger people inform their sexual lives as older adults?

I intentionally chose the people for this book to get beyond who I am, who I knew, and who I came out with.

As an aging, white, Jewish, lesbian-identified, activist, feminist, cis woman from New York, I wanted to expand beyond my own networks to dig into the lives of LGBTQ elders across the country, across the spectrum of identities, with more diversity than I could impart, and ask them how they would address these critical questions. The people whose stories populate the following pages face struggles arising from their sexual orientation, gender, race, ethnicity, religion, politics, disabilities, kinkiness, non-monogamy, and other identities.

I've added a postscript as an homage to the legacy of these LGBTQ elders from the eyes of a young gay man, Joey Wasserman, who recounts what he's learned from his elders and their political struggles. In the epilogue, I talk about what I've learned from this extraordinary group of people living through extraordinary times and what we still need to learn about the lives of LGBTQ elders in the Stonewall Generation.

I provide commentary to set the stage for each interview and introduce you to each of the elders at the start of each chapter. Yet the bulk of this book is composed of the words spoken to me in each of the interviews I conducted so you can get the flavor—regionally, culturally, and politically—directly in their voices.

You might hear stories that resonate with your own. You might learn how different each of these experiences is from yours. You might find a way to become an ally with an LGBTQ elder in your own life. There is pain. There is sadness. It is not always loving, even within the LGBTQ community. Lani Ka'ahumanu recounts the utter invisibility of bisexual people and the hostility she suffered from her lesbian friends. Mandy Carter speaks about the racism she endured. Hardy Haberman talks about the marginalization of people in the leather community. Imani Woody-Macko describes the racism and sexism, both visible and invisible, that she fights every day.

There are many more stories that need to be told. Just dive in and you'll see. What you're holding in your hands are the stories of those who were there, those whose lives were changed forever, and those who might never have changed the world had it not been for these moments. We need to hear these voices, particularly at a time when our country is in the middle of a crisis that could shatter hard-won, core values we've fought for over and over again in our nation's history.

WHERE DOES OUR STORY OF LGBTQ ACTIVISM BEGIN?

Some might say we should start at Stonewall in 1969. When I began writing this book, that's where I thought we'd start. The Stonewall Rebellion has been considered the birth of a new wave of a liberation movement that changed the world for millions of lesbians, gay men, bisexual people, drag queens, drag kings, and transgender people of all races, ethnicities, and ages. Yet it was certainly not the first raid nor the first moment of protest for LGBTQ people. The raid at Stonewall was preceded by decades of police harassment of establishments that served the LGBTQ community. The first recorded anti-gay raid of a bathhouse was in 1903, at the Ariston Hotel Baths at 55th and Broadway in New York, where dozens of men were arrested. Seven of them received sentences ranging from four to twenty years in prison. Countless raids, arrests, and imprisonments occurred in the decades that followed.

In 1959, at a place called Cooper Do-nuts in Los Angeles, a group of patrons generally described by historians as gay men and drag queens threw coffee, donuts, trash, and utensils when the police started rounding them up. Sometime in August 1966 (the exact date is unknown since there are no press reports), trans women fought back at Gene Compton's Cafeteria in the Tenderloin district in San Francisco. Trans people weren't allowed into many of the bars that catered primarily to gay men and Compton's was their chosen spot. Police were continually harassing them. In protest, one trans woman reportedly threw a cup of coffee in an officer's face, which ignited a riot and gave rise to an unprecedented moment of resistance to police violence. It was the first trans-led march for freedom ever recorded.

Stonewall was also preceded by extraordinary political activism abroad. In 1897 Berlin, Dr. Magnus Hirschfeld, a

> Trans women, including early activists like
> Miss Major, Marsha P. Johnson, and Sylvia
> Rivera (who were in New York) or Amanda
> St. Jaymes, Donna Personna, and Collette
> LeGrande (who were in San Francisco),
> generally didn't call themselves trans in
> those days. They were more often calling
> themselves drag queens. However, in the
> accounts written recently, historians have
> referred to Compton's as a trans protest
> (using current vernacular).

visionary, a socialist, and a gay Jewish doctor, started the Wissenschaftlich-humanitäres Komitee (or the Scientific-Humanitarian Committee), the first gay rights organization, which fought for the repeal of Paragraph 175, a law criminalizing male homosexual acts. (A proposal to add sex acts between women was debated in 1907 but never passed.) Hirschfeld was arguably the founder of the first LGBTQ rights movement. And in 1919, he founded the Institut für Sexualwissenschaft (loosely translated, the Institute for the Science of Sexuality). He opened and ran the Institute from 1919 to 1933 until the Nazis set fire to it. Hirschfeld supervised the first gender reassignment surgeries, performed by Dr. Ludwig Levy-Lenz and later

Kurt Warnekros. He published a well-respected medical journal and amassed a huge collection in his own library on a wide range of sexual behaviors. His activism and his scholarship were decried by the Nazis, who burned his vast library of materials, more than 20,000 books, in 1933. Though his library and Institute were destroyed, he became an inspiration to many others in Germany and across the ocean.

In 1924, Henry Gerber, a German immigrant to the United States, founded the first organization for homosexual people we know of in the U.S., in Chicago. It was short-lived but gave rise to other organizations. In the 1930s, Harry Hay, who had recently heard about Gerber's work, was an American trade unionist and Communist fighting for the rights of oppressed workers. Sixteen years after coming out, Hay, along with a small group of other gay men, began the Mattachine Society. It was incredibly dangerous to create an organization for the rights of gay people; it could have cost them their jobs, their housing, and their insurance. Earlier, they had set up the Mattachine Foundation as a more public discussion group based on the newly published Kinsey Report. Ideologically, the Society and the Foundation were quite different. The Society was more conservative and used an accommodationist mode, working with professionals to try to spread tolerance, dedicated to changing the laws that criminalized homosexuality. Hay was forced to resign in 1953 once

the Society started. Remember, it was the 1950s and Hay
was a Communist.

The Mattachine Society and Daughters of Bilitis generally avoided public protest in the 1950s under the threat
of Joseph McCarthy and political conservatism. Yet in
1965, the Mattachine Society of New York, Daughters of
Bilitis in New York, and the Janus Society of Philadelphia organized a White House picket line in Washington,
D.C., and Reminder Day protests in Philadelphia, marching as conservatively dressed and polite demonstrators—
men wearing shirts and ties and women wearing dresses,
but don't be fooled; these were extraordinarily courageous
and radical activists.

In the late 1960s, some small-scale changes were happening all over the world for gay, lesbian, and bisexual
people: After years of activism, Canada decriminalized
homosexuality, Poland decriminalized homosexual pros-
titution, and the Daughters of Bilitis formed a chapter in
Melbourne, Australia.

The political struggles of LGBTQ liberation of the
1960s came at a point in our nation's history when liberation movements were beginning to take root for African
Americans and women, a student-led anti-war movement
was igniting on college campuses, environmental movements were organizing consumers and workers, and the
sexual liberation, women's liberation, and civil rights
movements were fueling sexual freedom and basic human
rights from bedrooms to boardrooms.

At the same time, coming out, as you will hear from the people I've interviewed in this book, was not part of most gay or bisexual experience before Stonewall. Eric Marcus, author and podcaster of the astounding set of oral histories, *Making Gay History*, talked about the idea of coming out in a PBS documentary on Stonewall: "Before Stonewall, there was no such thing as coming out or being out. The very idea of being out, it was ludicrous. People talk about being in and out now. There was no out. There was just in." The idea of what "out" means has radically changed. Coming out used to mean becoming part of the "gay" world, not proclaiming your identity to the straight world. Many people (like Harry Hay) were very "out" in certain parts of their lives. There was a complexity to coming out back then that is not always understood today.

Though some of the people in this book were not directly involved at Stonewall, I use Stonewall as a moment in our history, a shorthand, and a flash of significance. With Stonewall begins the next part of our history.

There is a meaningful conversation happening now about whether "coming out" as a phrase applies to trans and nonbinary people, many of whom understand the process of disclosing their gender identities as coming *in* to themselves.

WHAT HAPPENED ON JUNE 28, 1969?

If you were around Christopher Street in the West Village in New York City, you might have seen or heard or been part of something unprecedented: lesbian, gay, bi, and trans people taking to the streets, fighting back against the police, defending their right to dance and be together and, yes, have sex. A truly historic moment and one that we can learn from today.

The mafia reportedly owned most of the bars in New York that catered to LGBTQ people, including Stonewall. Though homosexuality was legal in New York State, openly serving drinks to homosexual people and people presenting as a gender that didn't conform to their biological sex was deemed illegal by the New York State Liquor Authority (SLA), which considered bars like Stonewall to be "disorderly houses." The SLA either refused to grant liquor licenses to such bars or suspended or revoked many of their liquor licenses for "disorderly conduct." Without a liquor license, a bar couldn't do much business. The Genovese family controlled a majority of the "gay" bars in Greenwich Village, and one of the family members, Tony Lauria, known as "Fat Tony," purchased the Stonewall Inn in 1966 and turned it into a bar. Operating the Stonewall as a private club allowed him to get around the need for a liquor license. He gave bribes to the New York City Sixth Police Precinct of approximately $1,200 per month for the cops to ignore what was going on inside the bar.

And without much oversight, Fat Tony cut corners. There was no running water behind the bar, so the glasses were often used and dirty. There was no rear exit, which proved to be a problem the night of the rebellion when the cops were stuck inside. The alcohol was watered-down and yet customers had to pay higher prices for their drinks.

Given the bar's cozy relationship with the police, everyone in the bar knew the usual drill. Because it was an unlicensed club, the police would have had to get a search warrant to enter the bar to inspect the interior or shut it down for illegal activities such as sex or even dancing between members of the same sex). The bartender would usually get notice that someone from the NYPD would be showing up. Fearing public exposure and publicity, most of the patrons wouldn't resist arrest whenever police entered the bar.

Yet something different happened on June 28, 1969. On that night, two cops raided the bar at first. Deputy Inspector Seymour Pine was trying to end cooperation between the mob and the police, which is why there was no forewarning. Then a whole unit of cops raided the bar. Why so many? The plan was to take all the alcohol from the premises and make arrests, which required police vans.

Once the raid started, a crowd gathered in the little park across the street from the Stonewall. Someone threw a bottle. Someone else started shouting. The events of a chaotic late-night raid—an event that was all too common at that time—will always be hard to pinpoint exactly, even more so when records of that time were not kept. We may never know the full truth of what happened that night. But according to a *Village Voice* reporter who was there, the real turning point was when the police dragged a butch, mixed-race lesbian, Stormé DeLarverie, outside. Because the van was already full, they pushed her into one of the squad cars, but she got out. Three times. And tried to run back into the bar. Finally, one of the police pushed her back into the van and she yelled out, "Why don't you guys do something?" It was as if her question ignited the crowd.

Gay men, lesbians, and bisexual people fighting back? Drag queens and butch lesbians leading the charge? Proclaiming their identity? Not what anyone would have expected. At one point, the police were barricaded inside and couldn't get out (because there was no rear exit and the front door was blocked by the crowd from the street). Hours passed, and more and more people piled into the street. Fortunately, no shots were fired. The police never took out their revolvers or casualties would have been rampant. When the drag queens got into the vans, some of them created a kick line. Others chanted for their rights, and activists from other parts of New York joined in solidarity.

The riot lasted for a few nights in a row, died down, then flared up again a few days later.

Stonewall was not just a riot in the streets. Stonewall marked for many the bold beginnings of a militant resistance after years of criminalization, stigma, cruelty, and hiding. For anyone who was coming of age in the late 1960s or 1970s, people like me, Stonewall represented an opening, a door, a new beginning. A way out of the closet. That first night of Stonewall wasn't a pre-planned event. It was one of those spontaneous moments where all the pieces just fit. The next day, those who had been there on the first night organized to get people out for the second night. As I noted earlier, the Stonewall Rebellion occurred

Stonewall marked a time when women and Black, Indigenous, and other people of color were experiencing the liberating power that Stonewall opened up for people all over the U.S. Barbara and Beverly Smith, who helped found the Combahee River Collective in 1974, were feminists and lesbians. It was the first time in history that Black women openly and unapologetically communicated their sexual orientation as part of their social justice work, no longer trading silence for permission to engage in political struggle.

at the height of the anti-war movement, the Black liberation movement, the women's liberation movement, and other civil rights movements.

Organizing was going on all around that little tavern in the West Village. People who were there that night talk about it being their time. Time to take their movement to a new level. It was a spark at the right moment and created a new way to fight.

For consistency, it is at this moment in history that I began each of my interviews.

MY OWN STORY

I was in high school when the Stonewall Rebellion happened. It was a period in which my fellow students and I were writing and passing out an underground newspaper, with articles on women's right to orgasms alongside Huey Newton and the Black Panthers, Students for a Democratic Society, and the Vietnam War. We were going to rallies, eating hash brownies at parties, and having sex. All in that heady time. One of my bravest friends, Michael Hirsch, who was my first friend to die of AIDS in the 1980s, came out before the rest of us. He really was courageous. Of the small group of friends I spent time with, some were coming out then and some, like me, were trying desperately to stay in the closet—always knowing that something was awry, something was amiss, and something was really different about us. When I did come out a few years later, it was as if I was finally able to say who I was and be myself. That feeling of being an imposter that so many women feel? I felt like an imposter in my own sexuality.

And now, fifty years later, I am free to love the woman I choose, to live a life as an out and proud member of the LGBTQ community, and to make my living championing the rights of old people—of any sexual or gender identity—to live as fully sexual human beings. I write, I speak, I do podcasts, I talk on the radio, all of it about sex and older adults. I've written this book based on the stories of older people all over the country whose lives were incontrovertibly changed by Stonewall. They are gay and lesbian, bisexual and transgender, and they are getting older and grayer.

About the Interviewees

David Velasco Bermudez is a Stonewall veteran and a member of the Stonewall Rebellion Veterans Association (SVA), serving on the SVA's Executive Committee and as its liaison to Massachusetts. He has shared his story with groups around the country, providing a firsthand account of the Stonewall Rebellion. In 2015, he served as the grand marshal of the Boston Pride Parade. In 2016, David marched with the Cape Cod National Seashore division of the National Park Service to celebrate the naming of Stonewall as the first federal LGBT monument. He and his husband, Bob Isadore, live in Yarmouth Port, Massachusetts.

Mandy Carter is a Southern Black lesbian activist with a movement history of more than fifty years in social, racial, and LGBTQIA+ justice organizing. She is a co-founder of both Southerners on New Ground (SONG), an organization working toward intersectional liberation in the Southern states, and the National Black Justice Coalition. Mandy was one of the five national co-chairs of Obama LGBT Pride, the LGBT initiative of Barack Obama's historic 2008 presidential campaign. In 2012, she was inducted into the International Federation of Black Pride's Black LGBT Hall of Fame. Mandy is a co-editor of *We Have Not Been Moved: Resisting Racism and Militarism in 21st-Century America (2012).*

Edie Daly is the co-founder of Women's Energy Bank, a lesbian feminist organization that produced the feminist periodical *Womyn's Words* for more than thirty years. She also co-founded the St. Petersburg Salon, a monthly meeting place for lesbians in western Florida. She has worked as a global peace activist, traveling to Bosnia in 1993 and to the United Nation's Fourth World Conference on Women in Beijing in 1995. Edie is a member of Old Lesbians Organizing for Change (OLOC); Women in Black, a worldwide organization of women standing for peaceful and nonviolent conflict resolution; and Southerners On New Ground (SONG). She is the author of *Old Lesbian Memory Quilt: Stories Told By Edie Daly on Her 80th Birthday* (2019).

Miss Major Griffin-Gracy is a mother and grandmother figure to countless trans and nonbinary people around the world. She may be most well known as a survivor of the

Stonewall riots, but her ongoing activism has made her a beloved figure in her community of Black trans women and gender nonconforming people. Miss Major currently mentors trans women in the southern part of the US at her new project, House of GG, where she draws on her experience as a former sex worker and prisoner who survived both prison in Dannemora and Bellevue's psychiatric ward in the 1970s. At the outset of the HIV/AIDS crisis, she drove San Francisco's first needle exchange van, and went back into prisons and jails in California as a counselor to incarcerated trans and gender nonconforming people of color, as Director of the Transgender, Gender Variant, Intersex Justice Project. Her story is told in the documentary *MAJOR!* and her forthcoming book, due out in 2021.

Hardy Haberman is an author, activist, filmmaker, and sexuality educator. He is a well-known educator in the leather community and has presented at universities and kink events across North America. For his work, he was awarded the National Leather Association International's Man of the Year Award in 1999 and its Lifetime Achievement Award in 2007. He is currently the co-chair of the Board of Directors of the Woodhull Sexual Freedom Alliance, a nonprofit that advocates for sexual freedom as a human right. Haberman is the author of five books, including *Playing With Pain: Stories from My Life in Leather* and *Shouts in the Wilderness: Daily Meditations for*

Leatherfolk. His films include *Leather* (1996) and *Out of the Darkness: The Reality of SM* (2001).

Bob Isadore is a local political activist in Cape Cod, Massachusetts. He is the former chairman of the Yarmouth, Massachusetts Council on Aging, and former president of the Cape and Islands Democratic Council, which promotes Democratic political candidates in the Cape Cod region. Bob married his husband, David Bermudez, on June 27, 2004, the thirty-fifth anniversary of the Stonewall Rebellion. Five years later, he and David were on the float that led the New York Pride Parade on Stonewall's fortieth anniversary.

Lani Ka'ahumanu is a Kanaka Maoli feminist bisexual activist, writer, and safer sex educator. She is often regarded as the strategic political architect of the early US bisexual movement. She has a movement history of more than forty years, instigating and mobilizing social justice actions, campaigns, street theater, and cultural events while challenging bisexual invisibility and ignorance within the HIV/AIDS and health industries. She co-founded the first feminist bisexual political action group BiPOL (1983), San Francisco Bay Area Bisexual Network (1987), and BiNet USA (1987). Lani is the co-editor, with Loraine Hutchins, of the groundbreaking anthology *Bi Any Other Name: Bisexual People Speak Out* (1991). Her memoir, *My*

Grassroots Are Showing: Movement Stories, Speeches, and Special Affections, is forthcoming in 2021/2022.

Jackie Mirkin is a retired social worker and lesbian community activist. In 1955 she received a master's degree in social work at Wayne State University. She was employed locally and nationally as a Girl Scout professional staff member. Later she was a supervisor in a residential treatment center for adolescents, an assistant professor at Rutgers Graduate School of Social Work, and finally, a social worker in two urban New Jersey public school systems. Following retirement, she was active as a member of the New Jersey Women and AIDS Network, a staff member of the Rutgers AIDS Education Center, and a member of the Southerners on New Ground Steering Committee. Jackie and her wife, Edie Daly, were married in California in 2008. They are residents of Gulfport, Florida.

Imani Woody-Macko is a nationally recognized expert on inclusion and diversity, specializing in the field of aging and LGBTQ elder issues. She was appointed Commissioner to the Washington, D.C., Office of LGBTQ Affairs and to the mayor's Global Age-Friendly Task Force. As a veteran community organizer, Imani retired from AARP to start Mary's House for Older Adults, a nonprofit organization dedicated to serving LGBTQ elders experiencing housing insecurity and isolation. She has written countless articles on issues affecting women, LGBTQ elders, and people of color.

Joey Wasserman is the Senior Director of Development of SAGE, one of the oldest and largest non-profit organizations dedicated to the needs of older LGBT people. After graduating from York College in York, Pennsylvania, he worked in Washington, DC, for the Human Rights Campaign; for Dining Out for Life in Chicago; and as a consultant for various local and national LGBT rights organizations, including Freedom to Marry. He has also worked on Democratic political campaigns, including Senator Hillary Clinton's 2008 presidential run. He is a native of Philadelphia.

CHAPTER ONE

Sex Workers' Struggles

**Miss Major Griffin-Gracy,
born in Chicago in 1940**

Courtesy of Louis Shackleton

When I first heard Miss Major Griffin-Gracy speak, on a panel of elders at the National LGBTQ Task Force's Creating Change Conference in 2018, her poise and charisma were incredible. It wouldn't be hyperbole to say she stole the show. In a wheelchair and flanked by "her girls," she made quite an entrance a few minutes after the panel had officially begun. When Louis and I went to sit down with her for the interview and photo shoot, we had to wait our turn. She was surrounded by people who just wanted to have a moment with her, sneak in a hug, offer thanks. She was literally awash in love. A Stonewall

1

veteran, world-renowned civil rights advocate, revolutionary social justice luminary, and legendary elder, Miss Major
is a leader in the fight for trans justice. Generations of
trans women from all over the U.S. call her Mama. She has
a refreshing message of resilience and revolution.

Miss Major grew up in Chicago, has lived in New York
and San Francisco, and now resides in Little Rock, Arkan-
sas. She became politicized in the Clinton Correctional
Facility, a maximum-security state prison for men located
in Dannemora, New York, just after the 1971 Attica prison
uprising. For years she has been an advocate for trans
women in prison, and she recently retired from her position as the executive director of the Transgender Gender-
Variant and Intersex Justice Project, which focuses on
disproportionate incarceration of transgender people. She
is now working on a new project in Little Rock, the Griffin-
Gracy Educational Retreat and Historical Center, or, as
she likes to call it, The House of GGs, which their website
describes as a "safe and transformative space where members of the community can heal—physically, mentally,
emotionally, and spiritually—from the trauma arising from
generations of transphobia, racism, sexism, poverty, ableism
and violence, and nurture them into tomorrow's leaders."
The website also identifies the primary focus as "supporting and nurturing the leadership of Transgender women
of color living in the U.S. South." For the community, she
identifies as a Black elder transgender woman, but she told
me, with a laugh, "To myself and my sons and people who
are intimately close to me, I consider myself a man with
titties." (She said she always loved them and "wanted a pair

for myself.") Miss Major affectionately refers to the trans women she works with as her "girls" or "gurls" in a gentle, kind, and respectful way. She loves color and flair—and big entrances. She drives a 1960 Cadillac convertible with a license plate reading TSCUGR, "trans cougar." She is also the subject of an award-winning documentary feature film, MAJOR! by Annalise Ophelian and StormMiguel Florez.

As a sex worker in 1969, Miss Major arrived at the Stonewall at the end of a night of work to check on the safety of her girls. She was there the night of the uprising and has a rarely heard story to tell. She is one of the few remaining survivors of Stonewall, and her perspective on the uprising has too often been ignored.

THE NIGHT OF JUNE 28, 1969

I usually started working around midnight and then I got a ride downtown. I worked by the station up on Thirty-Fourth and Eighth Avenue. I just had to make a trick downtown, and then I went to Stonewall to meet some friends after work. Most of the girls had hooked, so they'd go by to have a drink, check on their friends to make sure they didn't get busted, and then go home. Stonewall was in the Village, and I lived uptown, off of Amsterdam Ave., but we still met down there.

As far as the incident at Stonewall, people have the tendency to think that it was some kind of planned event, or it was some kind of riot. It wasn't a riot! We were fighting for our fucking survival. Because at that time, you had to wear three articles of men's clothing if you were a trans woman [*or you could be arrested for crossdressing*]. You had to have three articles of women's clothing if you were a trans man. And the thing is that, as trans women, we are *way* more noticeable than trans men. What wound up happening was, it was just one of those nights when it wasn't going to happen like it usually had. Usually, when the cops came in, the nightstick hit the door jamb and you filed out. They were doing that to see what minors were in the bar and to harass us. And the bars were owned by those "questionable people," and so sometimes the police got paid [*i.e., bribed*] enough; sometimes they didn't. But sometimes, even if they did, they still came to the tranny bars and chased us out.

What happened that night was when the cops came in, they told us, "Get up and get out." But no one got up and no one got out and moved away. You know what I mean? And it was just a feeling of . . . things are different tonight. And you could feel it in the air. No one really said anything, you know? And on our way outside, we got into a fight, I don't know how it started. The rumor was someone threw a shoe or a beer bottle.

What I had learned in Chicago from fighting the police is, if you're in a confrontation with one, do something to piss him off, so he knocks you out, and then he'll step over you and engage the next person. But if you continue to fight him, he'll break your bones, shatter your jaw, you know what I mean? So I licked the guy's neck, I spit in his face, and he immediately knocked me out, and then he went to drag me to the paddy wagon, where a lot of the girls were. And then the girls decided to come *out* of the paddy wagon and they chased the police back *into* the bar. [*laughs*] That was pretty funny.

And thinking about it now, and reading all this stuff that's come out about it, and the books people have been writing, I have yet to see something written by one of the Black girls that were there. Because for most of us, it wasn't something, it wasn't monumental! That was a part of our lives! And we were fighting for our survival! We were fighting so we could live to see another day. This had nothing to do with politics. Or doing the right thing. Or standing up for our rights. No, no one let us know we had rights at the time.

THE TRUTH ABOUT STONEWALL

The thing about it, for me, after the fact, was it got white-washed and taken away from my girls and me. Because it was a bar for mostly trans women, gender-nonconforming people, the oddities of New York at the time. It was a lone little spot that Stonewall was at; it had a second floor for extracurricular activities. And it became a matter of where's my girls in this? You know? A lot of us didn't even know about the first parade that they had until we saw it on TV! Because they just cut us out!

And I've read it turned into a movement, so then let's give credit to the people who were there, who started this, you know? I'm not asking you to pat me on my back, or give me a thumbs up, but just to acknowledge—a thank you!

It seems wrong that, even today, Stonewall is propagated as a white male privileged event that started the gay movement. But as trans people, we're not gay. And so, when they started this LGBT thing, it's like, OK, T should be first! It was our club. And we went there. And we suffered the most beatings. And there weren't a lot of white guys that were fighting. Believe me, they're not going to get their faces hit, or fight! My community, we're pretty used to fighting. We're going to take our wigs off and kick some ass. Put my wig back on and go home. So it was a matter of taking this from us. They perpetuated what they wanted it to be.

GETTING POLITICIZED AT DANNEMORA

I was in Dannemora at the time that [*the Attica Uprising*] happened. I was just one of the girls, I was in my twenties and I got sent there for five years. And after the inmates took the prison over, they shipped most of the guys to Dannemora and put them in the hole, where I already was for slapping water on a cop. At the time, guards would just come up to your cell and put their dick on the bar. And because I'm a queen, I'm just supposed to suck

On September 9, 1971, an uprising began at the
Attica Correctional Facility in Attica, New York.
Tensions were already high because of racism
among the guards, overcrowding, unsanitary
conditions, and other abuses, and the news that
Black Panther leader George Jackson had been
killed in San Quentin Prison two weeks before
helped trigger a revolt. Almost half of the 2,200
inmates rose up, seizing control of the prison
and taking forty-two guards hostage. After four
days of negotiations, state police recaptured
the prison with tear gas and gunfire. Thirty-
three prisoners and ten correctional officers
and civilians died in the uprising and the final
assault; nearly all were shot by police. The
Attica Uprising has been viewed as one of
the most significant landmarks in the U.S.
prison reform movement. Big Black (1933–
2004), born Frank Smith, was a leader
in the uprising and was among the many
prisoners brutally tortured by guards in
the aftermath of the rebellion.

your dick? I don't know you! And you're not even cute! I
like fine boys, and you ain't it. They had just brought me
a little bucket of hot water to wash my face, so I threw it
on this guy. So I wound up in the hole.

The Stanford Prison Experiment was conducted by Philip Zimbardo, a psychology professor at Stanford University, in August 1971. Recruiting students as volunteers, he assigned half to play prisoners and half to play guards in a mock prison. The simulation was supposed to last two weeks, but the "guards" began abusing the "prisoners" within thirty-six hours, and a female graduate student (whom Zimbardo was dating and later married) finally succeeded in getting Zimbardo to curtail the experiment after six days. The findings of the study and early accounts of it have been widely disputed. Outrage at this and other abusive research (such as the Tuskegee syphilis experiment) led to restrictions on human sciences research and the creation of institutional review boards at all research facilities and universities.

So when they brought those guys from Attica in, I was there when they were beating them and torturing them. Putting cigarettes out on them. You could smell the burning flesh. The guards were so angry that someone challenged their authority. While the guys were there, I got to talk with them and become intimate with them. They didn't ostracize me because I was one of the girls. They talked to me straight up. And then Big Black helped me learn exactly what I was doing to protect my girls that I needed to take a step further. And he showed me exactly what the politics were. At the time, I'm just fighting for my girls' and my survival. I had no idea about the hypocrisy of what was going on. About the oppression that we were suffering from. About the prison system that was keeping little towns alive. People who hadn't even finished high school were making $50,000 a year to guard other people. And then I saw the study that they did at Stanford, about the prisoners and stuff, and it's like *Whoa, I'll be damned!*

SEX AND GENDER EXPRESSION IN HER YOUNGER YEARS

I love having sex. When you're younger, just starting off, you really don't know who you are. I remember being a teenager home with my sister. My parents would go out. I'd put on my mother's dress and run around the house. And I got bold one day and went onto the back porch. It had a screen and a wall. I went into the backyard and it was like this accomplishment, this major feat. Then I walked to the garage door, just swishing. Then I realized, oh my gosh, someone really could see me, and I ran back into the house. At the time, I was having sex with the boy who lived next door. And due to what the context was over masculinity and femininity, I was always sucking his

Christine Jorgensen (1926–1989) was one of the first Americans to publicly announce their transition and gender confirmation surgery. She was the subject of a front-page article in the *New York Daily News* on December 1, 1952, and published her autobiography in 1967.

dick. He always used to tell me I was pretty and all this other stuff. Then Christine Jorgensen hit the paper, and *Oh, I'm going to be the Black one of her.* Never got there, but I went to New York with that in my mind.

Got to New York and got my world turned upside down. I was still being submissive. I was hooking and giving guys blowjobs and stuff. And then one of the girls that I met taught me how to boost, how to flip guys when I'm in the car with them. She made me hip to hooking. So, after working, she and I would go to the bar and have a drink and go up to our apartment. She introduced me to this guy in this band, who played in a little club around the corner from where I lived. And I took him home, I got ready to suck his dick and then go to bed. And he said, "No, no, no. That's not what this is about! I'm here to service you!" "What you mean?" Baby, I haven't been the same *since*! "Oh! You can do this to *me*? Wait a minute!" So we didn't leave that apartment for five days. I had never fucked anybody I had been with, and I got to fuck him, and he fucked me, and we went in every room in the house. It was heaven. It was just heaven. What I learned about relationships in New York was, that was then, and he's never crossing that path again. At first I was like, oh, he doesn't like me, he doesn't love me. And then my girlfriend BB explained to me, "Oh, honey. That's just how it goes here. Now you just go find somebody and turn them out." OK! [*laughs*] And yeah, I've been on it ever since.

SEXUALITY IN HER SEVENTIES

Back in New York I had a male hustler who used to work on Fifth Avenue. I was complaining about not being able to find the right guys, and going to the clubs, and they either drink, or they're alcoholics, or they want to come home and take over and take charge and shit. There was another agency, before RentMen became popular, that the government shut down. And so RentMen is what I use now. And so, usually, for $200 an hour I get to pick what I want or he does what I need, or he can get the fuck out. So I've been using them. But lately, because of the changing times, there's been trans *men* advertising on there! Yeah, so now I have like nine penis-carrying guys, and four non-penis-carrying guys. Woo! Honey, like a pig in shit. [*laughs*] I be good. Not like those stupid-ass sites, where the guys are heavy, and they don't care for themselves. Because I'm a beauty, I'm sorry. I'm old, I'll be beauty, you be the beast. [*laughs*]

Miss Major serving as Community Grand Marshal for the 2014 Pride Parade in San Francisco. Courtesy of Quinn Dombrowski—flickr.com/photos/quinnanya/14560270363, CC BY-SA 2.0

WE'RE ALL CONNECTED TO ONE ANOTHER

Back then, it was a matter of telling my girls we're OK. Giving them someplace to stay, or helping them eat, or looking out for them when they're sick, because I believe that we're all connected to one another. We're family! And we lose family the moment that we tell them we're trans people. They immediately back up off us. Tell us to get out. Throw us into the street. Family's important! When the girls started calling me Mama, it was so wonderful that they thought of me in that way. I was just being a friend, trying to help them work through what they were going through. And now it's just grown exponentially. It's such a wonderful, wonderful thing. Right now, I'm the eldest, so I have to teach them what they need to be OK. And they have to teach the next generation. And it has to keep passing down! Because I'm not going to live forever! For what I started, I want it to keep going.

And so I'm on to Little Rock because I've had so many girls that I've known through the years that were from the South. They always had one or two family members who understood their journey and loved them anyway. You know, a grandmother, or an aunt, or a cousin. Always one, at least one person. And they always missed being home, to be near these people. And they liked the attitude of the South. The South is very comforting. It's like a big hug. And people give it to you who don't even know what they're doing. Because it's an atmosphere down there. My girls leave there, going to San Francisco or New York or LA to live a life. To get their hormones. To get their work done. To become the women that they see themselves as. And then once they've gotten that, they're afraid to go back home! "Oh, my grandmother hasn't seen me like this. I can't send her pictures because it'll upset the rest of the family." And so, my thought was, if I'm here you can come to see me, and I can go with you to talk to your family. Because I'm an older trans person, they won't see that I'm a trans person. I *always* have to tell them. Their relatives say, "Well, you're a woman. So why are you helping them?" Well, first of all, because I'm not a woman! [*laughs*]

And watch that face go . . . bloop! Yeah [*laughs*], I love that look. I say, all right, I got it, I'm good, right? Some of the girls start to say, "Oh, you're so pretty, you should do your hair, get your teeth done." I tell them, girl, I have teeth. They're in the other purse, in Little Rock. And the hair is folded up in my briefcase. [*laughs*]

THE TRANSGENDER GENDER-VARIANT & INTERSEX JUSTICE PROJECT

I retired from TGI because I have more things to do. I've been the face for TGI and prison reform for transgender women for fifteen, almost twenty years, and the agency has a good reputation. People like and respect me. And they are functioning and going on without me. I'm proud of them. They've taken it in their own direction, but that's what they're supposed to do! My dream for the future is the Griffin-Gracy Educational Research and Historical Center, the House of GGs. What I see in my mind is a compound with a library, so they can learn what their history is, who they are as a community, how far back we go, what the religious aspects are to us. Because we're in the Bible . . . as eunuchs! People don't talk about that! Where did all of this start? How far back does it really go? And so I'm trying to get fifty acres of land and then build on it. Maybe you're having a rough time in the cities. Maybe we can put up a little yurt or maybe a little trailer. And the girls can live there and do their thing. When they need me, they can come over to my house, and when they get tired of my ass, go back to where they're at.

I'm trying to get into a position to train the girls who are trying to do the work to make things better, the activists, first. Because they're having a hard time dealing with a lot of younger girls who feel as if the world owes them, that this is how it's always been. And until you realize whose shoulders you're standing on, you can't go forward. And so in teaching them, I want to give them the tools that they need to go back into their communities to work with the girls who have been giving them the hardest time. And then after I get them trained, then I'm going to bring in the people who are on the streets, to get them to understand why these people are trying to help them and what the pressures are. For me, it has to be grassroots! It has to be person-to-person-to-person.

One of these things that I keep in mind is the Highlander Center. I went there a couple of times, and they had their history of people being there: Martin Luther King was there, Rosa Parks was there. These are all straight people! I went there and it was OK. It wasn't for me! It wasn't comfortable. My trans girls are not a group of people you can sit twenty or thirty of us together and teach us. We've been fighting so long just to get respect for who we are individually, you can't teach us anything as a group. And then there's all this internal squabble over what's more important: being beautiful or being political. Passing or not passing. Oh, you're too tall! You're too heavy!

I've got to erase all of that. Accept the person that you're with for who they are and what their struggles are! And then share yours! Empathy has got to be employed into this so that we can move forward as a community. Suzanne

The Highlander Research and Education Center, in New Market, Tennessee, was founded in 1932 as the Highlander Folk School by Myles Horton, Don West, and James A. Dombrowski, who envisioned a place where Black and white workers could join together to learn about economic and social justice and organize for civil rights. White supremacists have attacked it twice, firebombing it in 1966 and burning it down in 2019, but it has persevered.

The Center was a key player in the civil rights movement of the 1950s and 1960s, hosting figures such as Rev. Martin Luther King Jr. and Rosa Parks at workshops and training sessions. It was the birthplace of the Southern Christian Leadership Council's Citizenship Education Program. Today the Highlander Center focuses on developing leadership and supporting those working for justice, equality, and sustainability. Suzanne Pharr, the Center's former executive director, is an organizer, strategist, educator, and author of many books, including *Homophobia: A Weapon of Sexism* (1988).

Pharr's been a big supporter of me. Keep it going, don't give it up, you know what I mean? A bit daunting.

PREVENTING SEXUAL VIOLENCE

Let me tell you about my girlfriend who died. She was murdered in her tub. In her own apartment. When the police broke in, she had two Rottweiler dogs that she raised from puppies. So the premise would be, whoever killed her, the dogs knew them. The dogs felt that this person was safe around her. So he had to kill her without any commotion, or killing the dogs, because they were sitting in the bathroom, and wouldn't let the *police* in! So she was a hooker! Check her clients! Look at them! Well, no. "She was a whore. And she got what she deserved." Pissed me off, got me going.

That's when I started having the girls who worked with me in the street do this. If you see one of the girls talking to someone in a car and she gets in it, write down the license number. If you can, casually walk by, get a look at him, and put a description with that license in your purse! Just in case. And then, when the police come, you have information to give them. The sad part was, even with that information, they didn't do anything! They said, "Yeah, that's too bad, sorry." Meanwhile, the police are picking us up for hooking, driving us to some parking lot somewhere, stripping off all of our clothes, making us suck their dick, and then telling us, "Well, get up on your own." It's tough. It's really tough.

TOGETHER IN OUR WOMANHOOD

When I was younger, I would have wanted someone to say, "I see what you're doing, let me help you." Because the two of us could cover more ground than I could cover by myself. What I would tell these girls today is, there's no need to be so angry and bitter. That kind of thing is consuming and you can get caught up in it and never get out of it. Because you won't see that it hasn't wrapped itself around you. And to be patient. Be loving. And be respectful of other people's point of view, position, and looks!

That's why sometimes I wear hair, sometimes I don't. Sometimes I run around with snaggles. [*laughs*] No, I'm not trying to be a glamour puss. I was when I was younger. I was cute then. But as an older person, dealing with these girls, with all the changes that are happening, all the things that they can do to fit this mold of what they think it's like to be a woman! And explain to them, you're not a female! You're never going to be a female, but you can have woman*hood*. And that's what we're a part of! We're a part of womanhood. And so we have to work together *in* our womanhood, to help other women who are a part of that. Whether they're a female or a male person!

CHAPTER TWO

Fighting Back

David Velasco Bermudez and Bob Isadore

Courtesy of Shana Sureck

Photographer Shana Sureck and I followed directions to a scenic, small town nestled on the coast of Cape Cod to interview David Bermudez and Bob Isadore. David had been the first person to reply to my call for people whose lives had been changed by having been at the Stonewall on that fateful night over fifty years ago. He was also the first person I interviewed, and I was a bit nervous, armed with an audio recorder and a long list of questions. Shana had her lights, camera, and lenses. We hauled our equipment out of the car to a small clapboard-shingled cottage. It looked lovely and compact, but as soon as we walked inside, we were overwhelmed. Antiques and adornments packed the place—small and large statues, oil paintings, decorative lamps, dried hydrangeas, farm tools—the best of David and Bob's antique dealer days. We could barely fit all of Shana's camera equipment in. For their portrait, David and Bob sat in front of a large wooden carving of a rabbit.

The interview was a lot like the house, filled with treasures and packed with history. David was delightful with his infectious laugh; Bob, supplementing stories of David's early activism, had his own charm and shine. They couldn't have been more generous with their time, their home, and their food (they're also wonderful cooks). They've been a couple since 1974. We sat down at their dining room table, David with his Stonewall baseball cap on, and talked for hours about being in the closet, coming out, fighting back at Stonewall, and their hopes for the future.

**David Velasco Bermudez,
born in New York City in 1940**

David was born on January 27, 1940, at Flower Fifth Avenue Hospital in Manhattan, and was brought up in the Bronx. His mother was from Puerto Rico. When his parents divorced, he went to live with his abuela in the Bronx and then to a big house in Jamaica, Queens, that had once belonged to Al Jolson. He lived there until he left home at age fifteen to go to Florida. He has worked as a singer, designer, and antiques dealer.

DAVID'S WIFE KNEW BEFORE HE DID

When I was younger, I got married to this girl, and she was very lovely. She and her mother lived in a house next door, and they were nice people. So I married her. I got married. And then about two or three years later, I went, *Something's wrong here.* And I couldn't understand what was happening to me. Remember, I'm from a Latin family. Father a minister, the whole bit. So I went ahead and I said, "We're gonna have to separate." "Why? Something wrong?" she said to me at that time. She said, "Are you a homosexual?" I says, "What's that?" But something was happening, I didn't know what it was.

COMING OUT AT THE LAUNDROMAT

Then I was living in a gay section of Columbus Circle and I didn't even know it. I used to go to a laundromat to wash all my clothes. There was a lot of guys and they were always saying hi and I'd go, "Hi, how are you?" And they'd go, "Fine, where you live? You gotta come visit" and all that. I didn't know they were all gay. So I didn't think anything of it, and you know how you sat on the stoops in summer and talked and all? There was this very cute guy who was sitting there. We were talking, and he says to me, "Are you gay?" And I went, "Gay? Well, what do you mean by 'gay'?" 'Cause at that time they had just started using the word *gay*.

And he says, "Well, you know, I was thinking of going to a psychiatrist."

"For what? I was married, I have a kid," I says. "So what?" he says. I went, "What's this? What's going on here?"

So he says, "We're gonna take care of this."

I was living in a gay section, and that's why the guys all liked me, because I was very friendly! I'd say, "Come on and visit me!" I didn't know what was going on. So we had about three or four gay guys. We'd go to bars. And I was presented to the gay bars in Greenwich Village and some of the gay bars on the East Side and the West Side, and there were a couple of Latin bars in the Bronx that we'd go to. And we go to the bars, and still nothing, And guys would always come at me and that was fine. "You want to dance?" "Yeah, I'll dance." But nothing else. I wouldn't do anything. So I got to know five real great friends. We stayed friends for years and years and years, until they all passed away. Most of them died of AIDS.

JUDY GARLAND'S DEATH BROUGHT HIM TO THE STONEWALL

It was in the summer. On West End Avenue there's a grassy area up there. We had a little portable radio and a blanket, and we'd lay there and get some sun. And the radio was on. It was Judy Garland, found dead in London. From an overdose. What? Judy Garland? So I got real nervous, and I went home, and I called some friends. They said, "Oh my God, oh my Lord"; we took it really bad. So we found out that Judy Garland in her will wanted to be laid out in Campbell's funeral parlor in New York City, where Rudy Valentino was laid out. That's what she wanted. And she loved the gay men because all her concerts were 99 percent gay men, and the Carnegie Hall Concert, she just loved gay men. And then I found out her father was gay! We never knew her father was gay. And then I found out her husbands were gay. You know?

Before she died, she used to come to Manhattan, when we were doing our plays, and we would go to this bar on Seventy-First St., between Columbus and West End. It was called the Penthouse. And we'd go there to have

Julius is a restaurant in Greenwich Village, just one block away from the Stonewall Inn. It's been called the oldest gay bar in New York City. On April 21, 1966, members of the Mattachine Society staged a "sip-in" to challenge the state liquor authority's contention that gay patrons were intrinsically "disorderly," its justification for revoking the licenses of bars that served them. They declared that they were homosexual and intended to remain "orderly," and asked to be served. Two other bars in the city gave them drinks anyway, but a bartender at Julius refused and the Mattachine members accordingly went to court. The New York City Human Rights Commission ultimately ruled that gay people had the right to peacefully assemble, including in bars, and to be served.

drinks and she always showed up! She always loved the guys, because she was always stone drunk. Either drunk or pills, whatever it was, always. But she was fun to us. We found this out and some friends of mine called me up and said to me, "David! Why don't we go out and have some drinks to celebrate Judy Garland's life?" "I don't do stuff like that. The woman died!" "No, no, no, we're doing this to celebrate." I says no. About 10:30 at night, I get a phone call again. "David, stop it. You're going with us. We're going to get on this train and we're going to West Fourth Street, and we're going to go to the bars and get ourselves drunk for her." "OK," I says. So we did, and as a matter of fact, I was just moving into a new apartment, so I had to be home to get ready, and I said, "OK, I'll give you a couple of hours." So we went. We went to all the bars. And it was unbelievable; they were full. People crying, music, it was really very, very hard for us. So while we were doing that, it was almost 1:00 A.M.! And I went, "Oh, I gotta get back! Guys, see you around. I'm getting on the subway. Anybody want to come with me?" Who gets on the subway alone? They said, "Come on, let's hit one more bar!" And I said, "No!" I think the last bar was Julius, by the way. And I said, "No, I've got to go back, you crazy?" "We'll help, we'll help you." I said, "OK, one more drink." You know I used to drink a lot of beer. We went to the Stonewall.

INSIDE THE STONEWALL ON JUNE 28, 1969

So here we are in Greenwich Village, us crazy guys. The Village was full of people. Got there late at night. Place was crowded, lots of music, the whole bit, a lot of crying, especially the queens. We went in, and when we got in, the Latinos always went to the back of the bar. When you go to the bar, in the back, there's a little booth there. We were always back there. The Latinos and sometimes the

Italian guys, but it was mostly Latino, so we were back there, and got our beers or whatever, and we were there, maybe, close to a half hour or something like that. And all of a sudden the doors were slammed open! And a bright light goes on. It was lights that used to go on, they used to say, "Hey," you know, "the police are here," and we saw these plainclothesmen coming in with a couple of police ladies in uniform. And they slammed the door and they said, "It's a raid!" And we went—excuse the word I'm gonna say—"Oh, shit! What's going on? I'm going to lose my job. I'm going to lose my apartment if I get arrested," and all that. So we were in the back. And you used to take out your ID, and you show your ID. And a lot of guys didn't have IDs so we used to, like, pass them on to them, you know what I mean? Just to help them out. And there were a lot of drag queens that night, and a lot of very, very young kids that were not supposed to be in there, but the doormen let them in. They were called street kids. They lived in the street, because parents used to throw their kids out and they lived in the street. So they were coming in, and they separated us! And these plainclothesmen came in, I think three of them, two ladies, I remember they were women in the uniform. And they were asking for ID, and we were in the back, and my friend he says, "Oh, let's get our ID out, and let's get the hell out of here. I've got to get out, I mean, we've got to get out of here." I said, "OK," so we were ready, we had our ID and all, and we were waiting. We were waiting there and all of a sudden we heard "Go fuck yourself, you dirty flatfoot." I mean, do I got to tell you how we New Yorkers talk? Especially with a riot or something? We went, "What's that?" And we didn't know! And we went, "Oh, God!" And I says, "Oh, Jesus, we're going to get arrested." And they said, "No, we're going to get out of here. Don't worry."

And before you knew it, somebody threw a chair. Before you knew it, somebody threw something else, and I went, "Whoa!" We were in the back looking at the front of the bar, where the doors were. And we didn't know what to do! And the cops, they were jumping on them, they were holding on to them, and you know, a lot of people don't know this but the gay world never, ever touched a policeman. They would come in, you give them the ID. They look at it, they didn't like you, they would throw you in a thing called a paddy wagon, they would bring you to the nearest precinct, book you, sometimes overnight. Mostly they did it to the drag queens and to the effeminate boys, because the boys would leave home, bring their makeup with them, and go in the bathroom and put on makeup even though they were boys. And maybe a little blouse. Those were called the effeminate boys. So they used to arrest them right away. Guys like us? "Get out! Get out, before I toss you out." But before you knew it there's this big thing happening there, and we were frightened! We were just like, *What is going on?* We still didn't know, but when I heard the dirty words, and I heard the "dirty flatfoot" and all, I went, "Oh, this is it," you know?

So we had to get out. So getting out, five of us, four guys and me. And we were trying to get out, and I'm coming out and somebody hits me on my neck with something. I don't know if it was a bat—you know they had billy clubs—or a bottle, I don't know. And I went, "Hey!" and I turned around, and I went to hit the guy, and it wasn't a cop! And I says, "What is wrong with you?" Didn't know, like I said, plainclothesmen were there! And it was one of them that hit me. So then when we were getting through, I was getting hit so hard we had to punch back and I swear to God it took like not even ten minutes, but it felt like five hours. Because of the yelling and the screaming and the cops were on top of people and all.

Williamson Henderson, who now runs SVA [*the Stonewall Veterans Association*] in New York City, was a very handsome boy. Everybody knew him because he had a car. And it was a 1969 Cadillac always parked outside. And everybody knew him that way. He was from the Island [*i.e., Long Island*], where there was probably rich little gay boys, I don't know. And I was getting out and there was a cigarette machine almost right next to the door, and here's Williamson on the floor and a cop on top of him with a billy club around his neck. And I looked at that and I went over to jump the cop, to grab the cop, and my friends were saying, "David! David! We've got to go!" and I'm going, "They're going to kill this guy!" "We don't care, we don't care, we've got to get out, we've got to get out." And here is Williamson, he's feisty and his dirty mouth and he didn't get the cop off, so . . . the doors opened. We went, "Whoa!" And we just pushed ourselves through after a while and got into the street.

THE SCENE OUTSIDE STONEWALL

When we got into the street it was late. It was very full of people because of Judy Garland's death. There was thousands of people on line for days. And they were all out there. All of a sudden cops and paddy wagons and stuff like that were coming. So, when I went outside, we were like that, and the people were saying, "Leave these guys alone!" They were saying that, the people! "Leave these guys alone," and all that stuff. And the cops were arresting and all. So all of a sudden I'm outside and I see this guy, this young boy—well, they were all young—took a garbage pail and lit it on fire. And then they took something and threw it through the window of the Stonewall, because they wanted to actually burn it. When the cops were coming out of the Stonewall, we were watching this. Thank God I wasn't inside; the kids went crazy. They wanted to hit them. So they ran into the Stonewall, the cops ran into the Stonewall! Pushed themselves in.

There was a young man walking by, and the cops thought he was gay. They grabbed him and they put him in the Stonewall with them while they went inside. The guy was a reporter for the *Village Voice*, which was not that far away. He reported that while they were in there, they were nervous. They didn't know what was going to happen, because it turned into a street riot. I always say that in the bar it was a rebellion. We rebelled. It wasn't a riot. But outside it was a riot. A real riot. So he said, later on, that while he was in there, the chief, Deputy Inspector Pine, told them that he was going to open up the doors and to pull their guns out and start shooting. Now, I was right in front of the door, where all our friends were. There was always a piece of wood against the window, covered in black, so you didn't look inside. But there was a crack and they would look through the crack to see what was going on. And he said, "I'm opening up the doors. When I open up the doors, fire." [*According to Howard Smith's reporting in the* Village Voice*, an unidentified police officer said, "We'll shoot the first motherfucker that comes through the door."*] We know about it because they—it was very weird that they grabbed the man, put him in the bar, and he was a reporter. So that was happening and they were looking through the crack and all that, and we were rioting, they were throwing bricks, because I think they were demolishing something. There was bricks all over. And there was little parking meters about so big, and so the queens picked up the meters and started running towards the door with the meters to smash the door in. And that's when the reporter heard, "When they open, shoot."

So when it was happening, I would have been killed. Because I was right in the front, like a lot of us. Pine heard the sirens and he heard the paddy wagons and he said, "Stop. Put your guns away." And when he went out there, there was already police and all that stuff. But if he didn't hear, if Pine did not hear that, we would have been shot. We would have been killed. And you know, through the years, we had get-togethers in Central Park with the policeman that raided Stonewall, Pine, until he died about four years ago.

REASONS FOR THE RAID

Pine was asked questions. "Why did you come into this bar and raid us? It was Judy Garland's funeral; we were celebrating for her funeral." Here's what he told us: At that time, John Lindsay was the mayor of New York City. And he wanted to get back in because he was losing the religious right. So he told cops to raid the bars. So Pine was into this religious right stuff at that time, and that's how he did it. He was into the religious right, he was going to raid these perverts, right? It's going to come out in the papers: "Mayor Lindsay got rid of the perverts." So Pine was saying that.

"Well, why did you do this? Why did you allow them to do this to us? Why didn't you just come on in and look around like you used to do?" Now the reason why he came in the way he did—and we knew it was more than just looking for us, because he came in, slammed the door, and yelled out, "Raid!" They never did that. They used to come in, walk around, push you around, "Faggot . . .

Queer . . . Give me your ID. Get out." So we knew at that time it was more than just looking around. And that's what he said. And a lot of the guys, they were very upset with him, and they said to him, "You have no right." Well, today I tell my friends when I talk, they did us a great favor. They did us the most fabulous favor ever. Yeah, excuse the expression, my ass was kicked; yeah, we were hurt; a lot of horrible things went on; but now, at my age, at this time of my life, thank you, Mr. Pine. Because if not, we don't know where we would be today in the LGBT world, you know?

See, another thing, too, with this happening: People forget even in the gay world that we had to go home. It was still not good. And we all thought that we were going have our doors knocked by the FBI or something, and we were going to get picked up and arrested. We all did. Because they had names and all that. So there was more fear after the rebellion. Because the guys that were there, I'm sure they'd ask, "Do you know him, do you know that," all that stuff. That day. They went to the Hudson and they threw themselves in the Hudson River.

SEX, AIDS, AND BOBBY

I knew these two guys that were very good friends of Mae West. Very wealthy guys, they were together thirty-something years. They admired me. I'll tell you why.

Every boy that came out was having sex with everybody. In the gay world, you had to pick somebody up to have sex with them. I always thought, "Well, let's go out and have dinner and drinks and all that." But in the gay world the boys pick each other up and they're screwing each other in the back alley! I was never like that, never. To me, the sex thing was not the important thing. Being Latin, being emotional in my own way, I wanted somebody that loved me and that I cared for, and we ate well, and we did things. You want to screw? We'll screw! But you know, hey, my life with you isn't . . . screwing all day! "Sorry, kid, we'll have our rice and beans and go home!" You know what I mean? So I was never that way! And even when I was a young man, so-called straight, going out with girls, I was never that way either. I found out, in the gay world, especially with Stonewall and all that, about the sex thing. And a lot of guys would meet me, and a lot of guys would want to do stuff, and I'd say, "No!" And they'd say, "Why?" and I'd say, "I just don't want to!" If we had a relationship and it was good, then it worked. I never, ever dated a guy to screw with him, or—like they used to do—go behind truck stops, and I knew all that stuff. I'd been to bathhouses, yes, gay bathhouses, but I wasn't there for sex. There was swimming pools, there was all kinds of stuff. And once in a while, ha, let's do it, let's get it over with. Now that I'm older, I love him. [gestures to Bob] I love this man for who he is and what he's done for me. Yes, Bobby is a very emotional and loving, loving man, but living with Bob, getting older, we show ourselves more love than just saying let's pull it, you know, and do our thing. And it's been hard for me, because we're getting up there. We love each other if we jump on a chandelier and swing with each other, or whatever. Yeah, we love each other that way. Right. We worked for this. We do this on our own. We have a *life*. Our life is beautiful things, friends, all that kind of stuff. Our life is not s-e-x. It's not that, I'm sorry. And if it was, probably me more than him, I wouldn't be here.

AIDS

The AIDS crisis did something to me that I thought it would never do. Number one, we were losing our friends, and we were scared! A lot of people didn't know where it came from. "Oh, maybe water," all that kind of crap, but we didn't know. And then one of the people who was living here with us all the time dies. Well, what's next? Bob and I were not promiscuous. We did not say, "Bobby, you go one way, I go another," like a lot of guys do. The AIDS virus hit and we were losing dear friends of ours. They were just dying. They were just dying, and we didn't know what the hell was going on. Then the sex thing became crazy. Is it [transmitted by] that, what you do and all that? And they find out, yeah, later on, yeah. More of the effeminate boys that liked the other type of sex, they're the ones that were getting it because of the blood or drugs or something like that. The same thing, and they're finding AIDS in the young kids. But they were going out and they were picking up stuff from other people and bringing it to their partner. A lot of people that we know who died, it was because their partner was out there with other people and coming back home. I know this guy who used to be the costume designer to Bette Midler and Cher. He worked for Bob Mackey designing costumes, and I remember one day we went to dinner at their place. We were talking and he says, "Let's do a toast." And he sat there, and I'll never forget this, and he says, "Through the grace of God, the four of us are here today." Because none of us were innocent.

When Ronnie [*David's first male lover*] died, I took it so bad that I stood in a friend of mine's apartment with him and I drank a bottle of aspirin. I wanted to die. And the thing that saved me was, remember the phones? My friend used to say, "Dave, I'm going to call you every hour." I say, "No, I'm all right. Don't worry about it." I heard a bell. I was hearing something and it was bothering me. He had called the cops. They came to the apartment, knocked on the door, I didn't open it. They smashed it in. And I was laying on the floor. And that's how he saved me. When I went into the hospital, they wanted to put me into either a mental institution in New York or in prison for two years.

So when I came to, I had tubes here. And this girl is sitting at the edge of my bed. And it was my sister! She heard this happened; she came in from Connecticut. And I looked at her, and I didn't recognize her until she says to me, "What's wrong with you?" I says to her, "You don't understand." She says, "What do you mean, I don't understand?" She says to me, "I've always known that you're gay, David. Even as a little boy." So I said to her right away, "So why didn't you tell me that before I got married?" And my sister was saying, "Yes, I did know. But, David, you're David. My husband and I thought of maybe going to you and saying don't get married, but you're David, so we didn't." When that happened, I made up my mind. After I got out of all that, I told my mother. I told everybody. So it got to the family. I just was left alone. Mi abuela I never told; she was too old. I think she would have understood it, because my grandmother was very together. I was never an effeminate boy. I just loved cleaning and I loved decorating. I'd say to her, "Can I help you cook?" And I don't know if that gave me away.

ADVICE TO YOUNG PEOPLE

If they don't like you because you're gay, or they don't like you because they're jealous of you, let it go! Let it go! If it doesn't come, it doesn't come! Just let it go! Don't get into it. Don't yell, don't scream, because time's too short. And I think I've learned that through life, being, like Bobby said, always very emotional and all that. I came from a Latin family—my father was a minister and all that. Not that they were bad people; my father was a good man. That's the world I came out of. And then, things happening that you don't expect. I'm a man just coming out. I lose the first person I love. To a suicide? Thank you, I don't think I want to be gay, you know? But I went on. And I—to this day we talk about this—I says, "Bobby, you know, I think we're together because we needed each other. We're together because we respect each other."

You know, I want to say something to you kids. I really want to say something to all of you, and we're talking about the Black kids, Latinos, all of you. If we don't all watch out, especially you guys, these things could come back. You know what we're saying? Oh yes, it could, it could. Our politics change like water. I know that a lot of you don't understand it because you go to your bars now and you dance, you take your shirts off, you do all that. I understand that. But somebody could start something. And I would say this, to all of them; I still say it when I talk. Because I feel through the years, if you do not get involved, and if you don't do something politically, and if you don't get involved with the LGBT movement, you don't get involved with the Black movement, and all that stuff, sorry, there's going to be some crazies out there that will get you. And that's going to happen; you'll always have that.

So I always remember that, and then all of a sudden, last year, or year before, this happens in Florida, the Orlando thing. When I heard it, my heart broke. And I said, "Oh, no." A little bar in Orlando. And to top it all, it was all Puerto Ricans. They were Latinos! Stonewall was a little bar in Greenwich Village with Latinos and Italians and Irish people and gays and lesbians. They came in, beat us up, did what they did. But I never thought in a million years it was going to happen again. I thought they were going to come in and punch you out. I never thought a man was going to come in with a rifle and shoot you down. And that really got to me so terribly. There's where we are now. It's not anymore "Let's get a billy club"; it's not anymore "Let's beat the hell out of them and call them fags," or whatever. "Let's kill them." That got to me. It was terrible. It was the most horrible day of my life. And I think, if you kids do not get involved and you don't get involved in your own little communities, have little committees, do anything, anything, get involved with each other, keep LGBT going—and now they call it LGBTQ—keep it going, because one day, some nut could come out and do something. This nut, with a gun, politically. The kids don't even know the McCarthy era. So this is where I am now with young kids. If you do not get involved, and

> On June 12, 2016, Pulse, an LGBTQ nightclub in Orlando, Florida, was hosting a Latin night when a shooter opened fire on those inside, killing forty-nine and wounding more than fifty. It was the deadliest shooting to date in modern U.S. history.

you do not protect each other, and you do not do things for each other and stop the screwing and the dancing, and start getting serious, I'm sorry, kids, maybe not ten years, maybe not twenty years, but it's going to happen. It happened in my lifetime! Here I am, in my seventies, and I see a man go into a bar just like Stonewall and shoot everybody down. And that's how I feel about the young kids! And when I see these young kids carrying on, "Oh, those things couldn't happen"—"Oh, really?" I said, because this is what's going to happen if you people do not listen and you do not do something for each other. And a lot of the young kids thank me. They come over, they thank me, and I say, "I'm glad you're thanking me, but it's not any good unless you do something about this."

GRATITUDE FOR STONEWALL

When Stonewall was happening, young people were fighting back because we were getting beat up and treated like filth. We fought back and said, "You've got to stop this, and if you don't stop it, we're going to fight you back," and we did. People see the years are passing and they say, "Oh, you're a Stonewall, oh, you're a hero!" "No I'm not!" "Yeah, you are!" We didn't think of that, we just thought, "Stay off our backs; if not, we're going to fight you back, even if you kill us, and all that." So now we're getting older, and I say, "Hey, you know, thank you!" Because look what happened! Look where we are. I don't think that it was some kind of a movement like Rosa Parks, that we would go as far, because when AIDS started, I was the first one to say, "There goes the closet. They opened it up again!" You know what I am saying? I feel, now, that I am alive and I'm seeing it growing, and I'm seeing our neighbors accepting. We can live in this, we can do this, we can do that. I mean there's a lot, a *lot*, more to go, you know what I mean? But I feel that through the years, the gay world took that Rosa Parks movement and brought it to us, and now we are growing because of that. We have a moment now to grow. Because what we crazy kids did [*laughs*], hitting cops and all, the ones that are alive, they go, "Pfft, we didn't think about all this kind of stuff." And the reason we are called Stonewall veterans is because we were the ones that were in the bar. We were not the ones outside. We were the ones that went, "Leave us alone!" I hope I live many, many more years, that I see the LGBT movement. And they're saying, "If it wasn't for you guys doing what you're doing, we wouldn't do this. We are coming out because you guys did this for us."

It was an awakening. I'm so proud to see what's happening with us. So proud. I'm living to marry my partner! After AIDS, you know? So look how far we have gone. But still, I'm very realistic; politics, things could happen. But we have to keep together, and we've got to help each other. Lesbians. All transgender. All. You know what I'm saying? We are a family, like that song, "We Are Family"? We are a family!

Bob Isadore, born in Fall River,
Massachusetts, in 1942

Bob Isadore was born to a Portuguese family in southeastern Massachusetts. He has worked as a buyer for large retail chains and as an antiques dealer. He is also an active leader in local politics, having been for fourteen years the first openly gay president of the Cape and Islands Democratic Council. Bob picked up where David left off, reminding us what it was like before Stonewall happened.

RECALLING THE BAD TIMES

They'd have their names and their addresses, where they worked! I mean, all this stuff was just put in the paper. These kids were either thrown out of their apartments or their families would throw them out. They'd lose their jobs. A couple of David's friends actually committed suicide.

MEETING NEIGHBORS AND
GETTING MARRIED

When we first moved here [*to Yarmouth Port, Massachusetts*], which was about twenty-one years ago, we bought this house. And there were no trees here, by the way. David's the one who planted all these things. It was all open. Here we are on a corner lot in a conservative town. David used to say to the neighbors, "Yeah, yeah, yeah, me and my brother bought this place." He was always calling me brother, brother. So one day the lady across the street came over and we're talking and she said, "David, my husband is a stonemason. He does a lot of jobs in Province-town and I've lived here all my life. Will you please drop the brother stuff? We know you're a couple."

We became really close to them. That started break-ing the barriers down. More for me than David. Because David was nervous because we're in a new area in New England, in conservative Yarmouth Port, and eventually we would have gotten it out there when they got to know us, but he was trying to . . . keep things. It was a nice rela-tionship but then, unfortunately, she passed away, when her son was only six years old. And the father went through a terrible time, drinking and all that. He used to actually leave his son, M., with us, perfectly knowing that we were gay, two gay men. They were that comfortable that he left the son here. So he'd go out, go on a date or whatever, and M. would be here and David would always tell him, "Well, you'd better be here by 10:00 because your son is not going to stay overnight here. Because we don't want any stories."

If the kid was sick at school, the nurse would call me and say, "Bob, he's not well." The father gave them per-mission, that if something happens, you call us. So I'd pick him up at school; I'd bring him home when he was sick.

He'd come here and David would say, "You can lay in bed, but if you feel sick you'd better get up, because Bob will kill you if you throw up in that bed."

That was it all the way up to the time that Dave and I were married. I told Frank and his new wife at that point, "Listen, we'd love to have you come to the wedding and all, it's up to you if you want M. here or not," because we didn't know how much, you know, it was a young boy, how much he could handle, although he knew we were gay. They said, "No, oh no, M. wants to be there." And when he came, the justice of the peace had asked if anybody wanted to say anything during the ceremony and M. raised his hand and he said, "Yeah," and he said, "I just wanted to say how much I love Bob and David, and they're like my big brothers, and I'm so happy they're able to get married." The father, you never know what comes out of Frank's mouth, says, "I know Bob and David all these years, and these two guys really deserve each other."

GROWING OLDER WITH DAVID

St. Jude is his [*gestures to David*] favorite patron saint. I said, "That's appropriate because he's the saint of the impossible." Perfect patron saint for David. Sex is part of the relationship. And we all feel that. But I, and I know David feels the same way, I think it's so much more than that. Besides the sex. I mean, it's part of loving someone. In some cases it's not, it's just . . . to have it. But as far as

I'm concerned, it's part of loving the person you're with. But a lot of it has to do with how our relationship has grown as we've gotten older.

GETTING POLITICAL

We weren't involved so much with the political when we were in California. It's only when we came back to Massachusetts, I encouraged him. I said, "Maybe you should start doing more with the gay community here." And by the same token, because he knew I liked politics, because I was involved in Bill Clinton's campaign in California, he said, "You should get involved, because you like that." We had both basically retired when we came here. I got involved in the local Democratic town committee and David was very supportive. It's strange because at that time, by myself, I was not as out as David was.

I joined my Democratic town committee here. We had a chairperson who left. She moved away. They were going to elect a new chairman and a few people said, "Bob, why don't you consider?" I said, "Eh, I don't know." I wasn't going to consider, but then we heard one of her remarks: "You can't have him run, because, you know, he's one of them." I said, "Now I'm running."

And David got right behind me, and he was there making phone calls. And when the election came, I won by one vote. One vote. That's a story I always tell the younger kids, that, number one, because it's your duty to vote,

Certificate of Recognition

I, Martin J. Walsh, Mayor of Boston,
do hereby recognize

David Velasco Bermudez

For your outstanding and creative efforts that raise both resources and awareness for LGBT rights. For advocating through STONEWALL Veterans Association, your Stonewall experience and participation, and through your love of music and the diverseness of the music industry.

The City of Boston congratulates David for being this year's Boston Pride Grand Marshal, and also wishes him and his husband Bob a very happy 41 years together.

Mayor of Boston
June 5, 2015

X-7130

THE WHITE HOUSE
WASHINGTON

April 25, 2014

Mr. David Velasco Bermudez
Yarmouth Port, Massachusetts

Dear David:

Thank you for your kind gifts. I was touched by your warm gesture.

At Stonewall, people joined together and declared they had seen enough injustice. While being beaten down, they stood up and challenged not only how the world saw them, but also how they saw themselves. History shows that once that spirit takes hold, little can stand in its way—so the riots gave way to protests, the protests gave way to a movement, and the movement gave way to a transformation that continues today.

Please know I am also grateful for your continued support for our shared values and vision for our Nation's future. Your generosity is much appreciated, and I wish you and Bob all the best.

Sincerely,

but in this struggle for equality, don't take everything for granted, because it's going to go away if you do. Ever since then, again, I was the first gay chairman of this organization and I've been reelected every year for fourteen years now. They won't let me go. [*laughs*] Then I decided to run for the Cape and Islands Democratic Council, which covers basically all of Cape Cod, Nantucket, and Martha's Vineyard. I was the first openly gay person ever to be elected to that position. I chose not to run for reelection next year. I have had congressmen call me and say, "Don't, please don't step down." I said, "Look, after all these years I need to. Somebody else has got to do it." But because of David's encouragement and because of my involvement in the political area, it's why I encourage some of the younger LGBT members to either run for office or get involved in politics. We now have a newly elected state senator in the Cape and Islands!

BACKING EACH OTHER UP

The same goes for David, where I get behind him; I say, look, you need to talk to the younger people. You need to talk to the school kids. A year and a half ago, the students voted to put in a bust of Harvey Milk at the local high school. We knew Harvey Milk in California, so I said that's wonderful. They wanted us to be at the dedication because of David being a Stonewall veteran and me being the first gay president of the Cape and Islands Democratic

Council, so we went. And I tell you, even to this day, I get a little lump in my throat walking up to Barnstable High School and seeing a pride flag flying over a public school for a whole month. I've never seen that before. And, for our generation, it's really like, "Oh, my god." And this younger generation says, "Oh, yeah, it's a Pride flag." And that's what we have to keep punching into their heads.

We walked into there, and it's in a courtyard, and there's a circular brick patio. We didn't know. In there they had put a brick: "David Velasco Bermudez, Stonewall Veteran." And next to it, they put a brick: "Bob Isadore, first gay president, Cape and Islands Democratic Council." That's going to be there forever. They've got a great gay–straight student alliance, but the fact is that this public school was able to fly the Pride flag for a month.

ADVICE TO A YOUNGER COMMUNITY

You have to get involved. You've got to do something. My involvement in politics, obviously I did what was right for the candidates that we support, but I also focused on LGBT issues, getting involved at the senior center, starting the LGBT program here on Cape Cod, and starting a hospice program for LGBT seniors.

The initial transgender bill that came up, I talked to a few of our transgender friends, and I was on the phone with the State House every day. I mean, I drove this man crazy. I was calling every legislator I knew, I was calling the governor's office, and people were saying, "Bob, why you? You're not transgender." I said, "No, but you know something? We need to be involved. It's a part of LGBT. You know what that means? It's not just gays or lesbians anymore. We have to support each other."

CHAPTER THREE

The Power of One

Mandy Carter, born in Albany, New York, in 1948

Courtesy of Bill Bamberger

I first met Mandy Carter in 2015, when she spoke at the Society for the Scientific Study of Sexuality conference in Albuquerque. She was listed as a social justice activist, and her talk was riveting. She galvanized the usually subdued audience into activism. I walked up to her at the end of her talk and asked if she was interested in speaking at other conferences, and she said, "Sure!" The next summer, I invited her to be the keynote speaker at a conference I was organizing with my colleagues from the Sexuality and Aging Consortium. I knew I liked her when she told me she was tired of giving

49

speeches and was wondering how I felt about us having a Q&A conversation instead. I was thrilled, and throughout the planning stage I grew to admire and respect her experience, instincts, and wisdom.

Though Mandy's formal schooling ended with her high school diploma, her lifelong education comes from over fifty years organizing and fighting for social change. She cofounded Southerners on New Ground (SONG), an organization working towards queer liberation in the Southern states, and the National Black Justice Coalition. She's done activist work all over the country. She has worked for Timothy Leary, Joan Baez, Roy Kepler, and David McReynolds, and also for Rikki Streicher, owner of Maud's Study in San Francisco, one of the oldest lesbian bars in the country. In 2005 she was among the thousand women collectively nominated by 1000 Women for the Nobel Peace Prize, an international initiative to increase the visibility of women's peace work around the world. She received the Susan J. Hyde Longevity Award in 2008 at the National LGBTQ Force's annual Creating Change Conference, and won the Woodhull Sexual Freedom Award in 2013. Today she is a member of the advisory board of the Tzedek Social Justice Fellowship in Asheville, North Carolina.

Mandy is one of the great super-connectors, embodying the "social" in social justice work and staying connected to both people and places. She helped me connect with Miss Major and also knows Edie, Jackie, and Lani. Her eyes are filled with light and hope, and her voice with determination. She identifies as an African American or Black lesbian.

Photographer Bill Bamberger and I conducted our interview and photo shoot with her at the home of Joanne Abel and Rama Mills in Durham, North Carolina. She told me that Joanne had had a role in hiring her at the War Resisters League–Southeast office in 1982. She moved from San Francisco to take the job and has lived in Durham ever since.

STARTING OUT IN LIFE ALONE

I was born November 2, 1948, in Albany, New York. Within a week of my birth our mother left me, my brother Ronnie, and my sister Delores and never returned. Our father tried to take care of us, but he couldn't, so he ended up going to jail for nonpayment. We were temporarily placed at St. Margaret's for Babies in Albany and then transferred to the Albany Children's Home Society for the next eight years. Then the Home got sold and all of the children had to be placed elsewhere. Because the Home wanted to keep all three of us together, we ended up being placed with Julia and Claude Minnisee, a Black foster family that owned their farm in Chatham Center, New York. I was eight years old when all three of us were placed there. But then my sister Delores got removed and sent to live at the Schenectady Children's Home in Schenectady, New York. And then I too was removed from there when I was twelve years old and got sent to the Schenectady Children's Home. It wasn't until I got my paperwork from the Schenectady Children's Home when I was thirty-two years old that I finally found out why we were both removed. I had gotten my period at twelve and the foster mother had me removed because she was concerned about me possibly getting pregnant. Our brother Ronnie ended up staying at the foster home until he turned eighteen.

I am most proud of going through the experiences of growing up in the two orphanages and the foster home for my first eighteen years. There are a lot of us who have and will continue to grow up in similar circumstances. While I didn't talk about my experience before, I am really glad to talk about it now. I do think that one of my biggest regrets was to have never found out why our mother, Emma Privott, abandoned us. She has since died. So I am using the Ancestry DNA kit and their website to do genealogical research on the Black Privott family in Edenton, North Carolina. I am also doing a concerted effort to find my brother Ronnie, who would be seventy-one, and my sister, who would be seventy-two, if they are both still alive.

LIBRARY RESEARCH

My coming-out process all started in my sophomore year at Mt. Pleasant High School in Schenectady, New York, in 1964 when I was sixteen. At that time for me, there wasn't any language for what I was feeling and thinking. And no one talked about it, but I knew that I was different. So I went to the card catalogs in our high school library to look in the "H" section for the word *homosexual*. And I kept waiting till no one was around, because I kept thinking that they would know that the only reason why I was there was to look up the word *homosexual*. Of course, I could have been looking for anything that started with the letter H. I finally found the cards for *homosexual*, and one of the cards was for the lesbian book *The Well of Loneliness*. I did notice that some of the cards looked a bit worn. So I thought I must not have been the only one looking at these cards. [*laughs*] It wasn't until 1966, when I turned eighteen, that I went down to New York City to go to this lesbian bar that I had heard about. I found it in a back alley, down these steps into a bar that was really dark. I do remember seeing women in either femme or butch dress. I remember thinking—this is it?

Something that I often say is "All you know is all you know." Until something comes along that's different for you, you're not aware. Being raised in the Albany Children's Home from age one to eight, and then being in the foster home from eight to twelve, and then from twelve to eighteen living at the Schenectady Children's Home, with foster parents who were Black farmers in upstate New York, I really didn't have a sense of any kind of racial identity.

Remember "Black Is Beautiful"? I wish I had that. I was the only Black cheerleader at the time. We were getting back on the bus after a game and someone yelled the

N-word to me. I looked around and said, "Who are you talking to?" One of my other cheerleader friends says, "He's talking about you, Mandy." See what I mean? During my formative years, I was raised for fourteen years in two predominantly white orphanages. And a Black foster home for four years. So no, I wasn't raised in a traditional "Black" family.

THE POWER OF ONE

I really did good at school. The people at the Schenectady Children's Home told me that if I wanted to go to college, they would pay for it. But by then something else had happened that interrupted those plans. Jack Hickey, my social studies teacher at Mt. Pleasant, brought in this young white staffer from a group that I had never heard of before, the American Friends Service Committee. That one forty-minute class changed my life. This is 1966. Think about what was happening at that time. Remember the Cuban missile crisis? Remember President Kennedy being assassinated? The young AFSC staff person said that while AFSC was a predominantly white peace group, they wanted to be an ally in and for the civil rights movement. He then gave us the history of the Quakers.

And then he talked about the power of one. He said, "Each and every one of us has a moral compass. And because of that, each and every one of us has the potential to impact change." But it was the last thing that he said that was the game changer. He said that they had an AFSC high school work camp up in the Pocono Mountains of Pennsylvania and wanted to know if anyone would like to go. I did want to go and got permission from the Home. At the AFSC camp they brought in a number of resource people. Who did they bring in? Guy and Candie Carawan of the Highlander Center. They called themselves cultural workers. I had never heard those words before.

Bayard Rustin, a heroic figure in the civil rights movement, was also a gay man. He helped found the Southern Christian Leadership Conference and was the chief strategist for Dr. Martin Luther King's 1963 March on Washington for Jobs and Freedom, which brought a quarter of a million people to the Capitol Mall. As a Black gay activist, Rustin faced many challenges both within and outside the civil rights movement. He was arrested numerous times as a civil rights protestor, for refusing military service in World War II, and for "sexual vagrancy" (for which he once spent sixty days in a California jail). One of his most famous remarks is "We need, in every community, a group of angelic troublemakers."

They shared that they were traveling in the South recording the freedom songs of the civil rights movement and
recording the meetings being held in the Black churches.
Their recordings are on the Smithsonian record label. At
the camp that summer, it was the very first time I had
heard the name Bayard Rustin. And it was the first time
that I had heard the word *gay*. That AFSC camp marked
another defining moment of my life.

THE SUMMER OF 1967

In 1967 I spent the summer in New York City. I took a
Greyhound bus down from Schenectady, New York, with
the eighty dollars that I had saved up from working as a
house parent at the Schenectady Children's Home. And
while I didn't know anyone in New York City, I was very
independent, and I was determined to make it on my
own. For the first two weeks I lived in a YWCA while I
looked for work as a cashier at one of the local grocery
stores. But I wasn't able to find any work, and I realized
that I wasn't going to be able to afford to keep staying at
the YWCA. So I packed all of my belongings into my
duffel bag and took it and my sleeping bag and moved out
of the YWCA and started staying in Central Park. A lot
of other people were also sleeping in Central Park that
summer, so it seemed like a safe place for me to stay. I
would spend my days in the park or walking around other
parts of the city. At some point that summer I decided to

switch from staying and sleeping in Central Park to staying and sleeping in the Village. On my walk downtown, I was on Hudson Street near the Village and saw a sign in a storefront window for the League for Spiritual Discovery that said "free lunch." I was really hungry, so I went in and had lunch. As it turned out, that particular day would end up being a major turning point in my life. The storefront was run by Timothy Leary. He and Richard Alpert popularized LSD, acid. The two people who were running the storefront were looking for someone who could work the 8:00 P.M. to 8:00 A.M. shift to answer the phone calls from people who were having bad trips on acid, to let them know that they could come down from bad trips by taking niacin, or vitamin B. It turns out it was one of the best summers of my life.

"WE DON'T SERVE NO COLORED PEOPLE HERE"

In 1967 the Summer of Love was happening. And my amazing summer in New York City was also coming to an end. So I asked my Japanese friend Toshi and my white friend Natalia if they wanted to hitchhike out to San Francisco with me. I said, "Let's go. Let's hitchhike out to San Francisco." So we did. At that time everyone was hitchhiking, so it was really safe. We started by getting through the Holland Tunnel into New Jersey. I said, "Let's stop at this truck stop and get some sandwiches."

We go into the restaurant and we go up to the counter. The white gentleman looks at me, looks at Toshi. And, then he looks at Natalia and says to her, "I'll serve her. We don't serve no *colored* people in here." We all looked at each other and said, "You're kidding, right?" He said, "Do you see any colored people in here?" I did notice the Black man behind the counter doing dishes. We were stunned. This place was only a tunnel ride away from the most diverse city in this country.

As we continue hitchhiking across the country, we get to Chicago. And now we are in a predominantly Black section of Chicago when we see a barbeque place. We walk into the restaurant and we all say that we're going to get some good barbeque here. We go up to the counter and the Black gentleman behind the counter looks at me, looks at Toshi, and looks at Natalia. He then says to me, "I'll serve you and him. We don't serve to no white people in here." We looked at each other, stunned once again by what we were hearing. Remembering that those were the exact same words that we heard back in New Jersey. That was one of the most defining moments of my life. Think about it. They both said the exact same thing. Having all three of us share those two experiences made us see and feel what is like to be the other.

On reflection, being in New York City that summer was more of a cultural experience for me. The awareness of race and class wouldn't happen for me until I moved to San Francisco.

GETTING CONNECTED TO ACTIVISM

Remember that song by Scott McKenzie, "If You're Going to San Francisco"? We found out later that he had been commissioned to do that song. Because so many people were moving to San Francisco that summer, the song was meant to create a positive, mellow mood. So for the three of us, every place that we stopped at that had a jukebox, we always played that song. I love that song!

Once we were in San Francisco we went to the Haight-Ashbury Switchboard, where people could find temporary places to stay. The Switchboard had Rolodex card files of people offering housing. The Rolodex card they picked for us was that of Vincent O'Connor at 531 Waller Street. All three of us stayed there for a while. Toshi and Natalia ended up going their own ways. It turns out that Vincent was a Vietnam War draft resister who worked at the Catholic Peace Fellowship. I ended up doing volunteer work for him there. When he got invited to a working session down at the Institute for the Study of Nonviolence, I got to go with him. It was a planning session in preparation for the first-ever nonviolent civil disobedience action at the Army Induction Center in Oakland, California, during the national Stop the Draft Week. That's who got me to the War Resisters League, where I was hired in 1969. Here's another connection. Bayard Rustin was the head of the War Resisters League. And several of the WRL staff who were working there were gay.

COMING OUT AND COMING HOME TO MAUD'S LESBIAN BAR

When I got to San Francisco I was not yet twenty. You had to be twenty-one to get into the bars. I found the lesbian bar called Maud's, located at 937 Cole Street. So you know what I did? I sat across the street from the bar, on a stoop, watching people go in and out. And the night when I turned twenty-one, I went into Maud's. But the next day, when they said, "Oh, you know we're open from noon to 2:00 A.M.," I said, "You're open during the *day*? You mean, you can walk around?" That changed everything. That's when I realized you all can be *out* here. During the day. Not like that dark alley at that bar in New York, coming around the back. An upside for me about my own coming out is that I didn't have any parents to be accountable to. I didn't fully appreciate and realize that until I was talking to friends who would say, "Oh, I can't come out because of my parents and what they would think and what they would say." Now that I look back at my own coming-out process, I realize that for me, I had to come out to myself first. And then I could come out to other people. And one of the things that made my being out that much easier was living in San Francisco that was so gay and lesbian. What was happening in San Francisco in 1967 was amazing. So many gays and lesbians were moving there from outside the area, and the number of lesbian bars, and it's such a small town. That's the first time I heard the L-word. Not *gay*! But it was during the day. In daylight.

Then I started learning more about Rikki Streicher, owner of Maud's. Turns out that she was adopted. So we had that in common. At one point I was getting a drink and Rikki said to me, "You want to know something about this bar? Anyone could go to a local store and get alcohol or beer and drink in their house. Why do they go to the bar, do you think, Mandy?" She said, "They come here because they feel like they can be a part of something that identifies themselves as who they are."

Rikki would say that "every holiday we are going to have a holiday meal here at the bar for those who have no place to go. Either because they can't go home because they aren't out to their parents or family, or because they couldn't get home." And when you think about everyone who came out at Maud's, or who went there, and you look at where they are, at the lineage of the leaders of our movement—some of our first [openly] trans people were at the first Maud's reunions. They were lesbians, they came

Like the New York State Liquor Authority, the California Department of Alcoholic Beverage Control (ABC) harassed LGBTQ people and their watering holes, considering them "disorderly persons" or "persons of ill repute." A number of sources say the ABC was created to harass LGBTQ people.

back as trans, and they were welcome. So, whatever it was that Rikki had, it was just—yeah!

In order for a bar to get a liquor license in San Francisco you had to go through the ABC, the Alcoholic Beverage Control Department. And given the ever-growing number of gay and lesbian bars in San Francisco, a number of these bar owners, including Rikki, got together and formed the San Francisco Tavern Guild. The Tavern Guild was an association of gay bar owners and liquor wholesalers that formed in 1962 and lasted through 1995. It was the very first gay business association in the country, formed in response to rising tensions between the police and the gay community. The ABC, with their initial anti-gay policies, had their own set of rules, that included no same-gender dancing or anyone visibly touching each other. In addition to getting liquor licenses, it [*the Tavern Guild*] also meant working with the San Francisco vendors who provided and serviced the bars' juke boxes, pool tables, pinball, and cigarette machines. And while there may have been an initial reluctance on their part to [*do business with*] the ever-growing number of gay and lesbian bars, it didn't take long for them to realize just how much revenue our gay and lesbian bars were going to generate. So the creation of the San Francisco Tavern Guild was a game-changer, both economically and politically. Not only was Rikki savvy about the San Francisco Tavern Guild, she also wanted to support what was going on in San Francisco City Hall. There was [*in Maud's*] a picture of Mayor Dianne Feinstein giving Rikki Streicher an award.

BEING BLACK AND BEING LESBIAN

Being Black and being a lesbian in the bars of San Francisco was interesting. At one point there were twelve lesbian bars. There were lesbian bars in the East Bay too, but unless you had a car you couldn't get over there. In the East Bay, particularly in Oakland, there were more people of color. That's why I'm intrigued about Stonewall, when I hear the stories of what really happened and who was really there. What I saw of gay and lesbian San Francisco was majority white. Occasionally women of color would come into Maud's. And then I found out that there were women who said, "No, we don't go into San Francisco. We stay in Oakland." They had a bar. It wasn't, like, a Black-owned bar, but Black lesbians—I don't think they even used the word *Black* at that point—were there. And for the handful of us who were at Maud's, they said, "Well, do you feel comfortable in here?" In fact, Pat Parker—she and I were close—challenged me one day: "I don't think you're Black enough, Mandy." She said, "You

Pat Parker was an African American lesbian feminist poet involved with the Black Panther movement. In 1978 she was part of Varied Voices of Black Women, an Olivia Records tour, with musicians Gwen Avery, Mary Watkins, Linda Tillery, and others.

don't talk Black." When I gave her my story, she said, "You're not Black." We were really good friends. She hung out in Maud's, but she also hung out in the East Bay.

I self-identify as an out Black lesbian. So when I moved to Durham, North Carolina, in 1982, one of the first things I took note of was the deep, rich history of the Black community here. I saw the names of Alston Avenue and Shepherd Street. These are named after Black families here. Durham is home to North Carolina Central University, that's NCCU, one of North Carolina's eleven historically Black colleges and universities, or HBCUs. Durham is also home to the North Carolina Mutual Insurance Company, the oldest Black-owned insurance company in the country.

So what does that mean if you are Black lesbian, gay, bisexual, transgender, and same gender loving, living in Durham? What does it mean to be living at the intersection of your race/ethnicity and your sexual orientation and gender identity? I know that there are Black lesbian house parties in Durham where you don't have to "come out" but can still be with other Black lesbians. There are Durham Black LGBT folks who will go out of town to be with other Black LGBT folks, but not in Durham, where someone might recognize them or members of their family. But there is good news, because NCCU now has its own LGBT and Allies campus group. There is the Durham LGBTQ Center located near downtown Durham. There is El Centro Hispano, that has its own Latinx LGBTQ group. There is the Imani MCC and Unitarian

Most Unitarian Universalist (UU) congregations have completed a Welcoming Congregation program to increase understanding and inclusion of LGBTQ people and their families and extend their advocacy beyond the congregation. UU congregations have called and ordained openly LGBTQ ministers for many years, starting in 1979. In 2019, Unitarian Universalists celebrated five transgender candidates called to settled ministry in UU congregations, the most ever in one year. UU ministers officiated at religious marriages of same-sex couples as far back as the late 1960s, and the Unitarian Universalist Association was at the forefront of the marriage equality movement. In 2004, UUA President Rev. William G. Sinkford officiated at the wedding of the lead plaintiffs in the *Goodridge* case, which resulted in the legalization of same-sex marriage in Massachusetts. Side with Love, a faith-based public advocacy campaign sponsored by the Unitarian Universalist Association, works to counter identity-based oppression.

Universalists, who are open and affirming churches.
And there are numerous companies who have their own
LGBTQ employee groups. Which means that there is the
option to come out and be out if that is what people of
color who are LGBTQ choose to do. And, nationally, there
is the National Black Justice Coalition that I had the good
fortune to be one of the co-founders of in 2003. NBJC
is the leading national Black LGBTQ/SGL civil rights
organization dedicated to empowering Black lesbian,
gay, bisexual, transgender, and same gender loving (SGL)
people. NBJC's mission is to end racism, homophobia, and
anti-LGBTQ/SGL bias and stigma. NBJC provides leadership at the intersection of our national civil rights groups
and LGBTQ/SGL organizations.

IF IT HADN'T BEEN FOR THE DRAG QUEENS

I remember when we had our first-ever official Durham
Gay and Lesbian March in 1986, down Ninth Street here
in Durham. At our very first organizing meeting, there
was the inevitable question and debate as to whether we
were going to have drag queens marching and performing on the stage. The anti–drag queen position being that
they don't adequately represent us. Or that's all the media
coverage will be about. Or what will the straight community think about us if "they" are representing us? Fortunately, the final and overwhelming decision was made

when someone said we wouldn't even have a gay and lesbian movement if it had not been for the drag queens! With all of us being reminded of the 1969 Stonewall riots in New York City, where it was drag queens and drag kings of color on the front lines, and being reminded how the San Francisco Imperial Court of drag queens partnered with the San Francisco Pride Parade in its early beginnings. And being reminded of our own drag queen culture here in the South.

In 2019, the annual San Francisco LGBT Pride Parade will mark its forty-ninth anniversary. It now draws 1.1 million visitors to its two-day weekend events, with over two hundred groups participating. It always kicks off at the San Francisco Ferry Building with the Dykes on Bikes up Market Street and ends in the San Francisco Civic Center, where there are twenty community stages of entertainment. So it is important to remember its beginnings. The very first event on June 28, 1970, centered on a small "Gay-In" in Golden Gate Park and a march down Polk Street—including drag queens. It was one year after the Stonewall riots in New York City. On June 25, 1973, a float appeared at the first San Francisco Gay Pride Parade. The rainbow flag identified with the LGBT community was originally created by Gilbert Baker for the 1978 San Francisco Pride Parade. So that in itself started the change of how our gay and lesbian communities interacted with each other. It also helped lay down the foundation for what would go on to be our annual San Francisco LGBT

New York City's first Pride parade—then called the Christopher Street Liberation Day March—was held on June 28, 1970, one year after the Stonewall Rebellion. It was planned by a committee under the leadership of bisexual activist Brenda Howard. On the same weekend on the West Coast, San Francisco had a "Gay In" in Golden Gate Park and Los Angeles held the nation's first officially permitted Pride parade, called "Christopher Street West Pride." However, the claim to fame for the first Pride parade in the country goes to Chicago, as they held their first "Gay Liberation March" the day before, on June 27, 1970.

Pride parades and festivals. Thanks to Rikki Streicher and her two lesbian bars, Maud's and Amelia's, we formed the San Francisco Bay Area Women's Float Committee and had the first-ever women's float in the 1980 San Francisco Pride Parade.

When I first moved to San Francisco I was in awe of the huge gay and lesbian communities. I was struck by how little our gay and lesbian communities really interacted with each other. But, because of an ABC rule about who could be bartenders in our gay and lesbian bars it ended up having a very positive impact. Another rule of the ABC was that unless you owned your bar, women were not allowed to be bartenders. But because Rikki owned Maud's, she could be behind the bar serving drinks. So who did she hire to be bartenders? The gay male bartenders from the Castro gay men's bars! So that in itself changed the way we interacted with each other.

GETTING ARRESTED FOR THE FIRST TIME

I found out about the War Resisters League when I visited the Institute for the Study of Nonviolence earlier that summer. The two groups were going to have their first-ever nonviolent civil disobedience [CD] action at the Oakland Induction Center in October 1967, during the national Stop the Draft Week. They were looking for people to participate in the CD action. I ended up going to a second CD action that December and got arrested. While I was in jail at the Santa Rita Prison Farm, Jane Schulman, another woman who also got arrested at the Oakland Induction Center, came up to me and said, "Have you ever heard of the War Resisters League?" I said, "Yes, when I visited the Institute." She said, "Well, I want to let you know that we're having a potluck at our WRL office. Would you like to come?" I went to their potlucks. Those potlucks led to mailings, and the mailings led to my participating in their other WRL activities. Then Randy Kehler, who was also on the staff there, ended up going to jail for being a draft resister. They had to fill his staff spot and they offered it to me. So that is how

I got my first-ever job in the movement, at WRL-West. This is also the same Randy Kehler who played a pivotal role in his impact on Daniel Ellsberg when Dan heard him speak at a college lecture. It would be Daniel Ellsberg who would later release the Pentagon Papers in opposition to the Vietnam War.

THE MURDER OF HARVEY MILK

There had been word that Harvey Milk wanted to run for San Francisco supervisor. Everyone knew his camera store on Castro Street and where it was. For me, my initial reaction was, why? I thought everything was good with our gay and lesbian community just as it was. Did we need a gay supervisor down at San Francisco City Hall? But on that fateful day of November 27, 1978, when Harvey Milk and Mayor George Moscone were murdered at City Hall by Dan White, that changed everything. Word went out that everyone was to meet at the corner of Castro and Market, to bring a candle, and walk in silence down to City Hall. It is a moment that I will never forget. Because at that moment it was the first time ever that I can remember when our gay and lesbian community came together. I remember saying to myself, What have we been doing? Why did it take these senseless murders to bring our community together to understand that yes, it does make a difference to be represented in City Hall? That this is what Harvey was talking about?

Harvey Milk's camera shop on Castro Street was a gathering place for the gay community. After two unsuccessful runs for the office, he was elected to the San Francisco Board of Supervisors in 1977, becoming one of the very few openly LGBTQ elected officials in the country. He served almost eleven months in office, during which time he sponsored a bill banning discrimination in public accommodations, housing, and employment on the basis of sexual orientation that passed by one vote. Dan White, another supervisor, was an outspoken opponent of Milk and the LGBTQ community. White resigned from the Board of Supervisors on November 10 but almost immediately tried to withdraw his resignation; however, Mayor George Moscone was unwilling to reappoint him. On November 27, White entered City Hall through a window and shot first Moscone and then Milk to death in their offices.

CRUISING AND WORKING
AT THE LESBIAN BARS

As for sex, well, not that much for me. I could count on one hand the number of women I have been with! [*laughs*] As a bartender at both Maud's and Amelia's, I got to see firsthand lots of the interactions with our lesbian customers. At Maud's, whenever the front door would open everyone sitting at the bar would turn to see who was coming in. Sitting at the bar, if you wanted to get another woman's attention that you might be interested in, you would send her a drink and let her know that it came from you. I remember one time when I was bartending, a woman walked into Maud's, took one look, and said, "I've been with every woman in this bar. Well, I guess it's time to start over again!" And then there were the phone calls that I would get at the bar. The woman on the phone would ask—I love this—if her girlfriend was there. She would say, "Is Mary there?" Meanwhile, Mary is sitting at the bar right in front of me and would wave me off. And I'd have to say, "No, she's not here, haven't seen her!" Just things like that. [*laughs*] Things like that were just part of the lesbian bar culture. Some would call it cruising. Women would be in the bars to drink, to dance, play pool, and maybe hook up or not. When Rikki opened up Amelia's at 647 Valencia Street, it was the biggest thing at the time. It was one of the first lesbian dance bars in the city, while Maud's was always the nice neighborhood bar that we

Tom Waddell was a gay athlete who died of HIV/AIDS in 1987. He placed sixth in the decathlon at the 1968 Mexico City Summer Olympics, suffered a knee injury during a high jump event at a 1972 Hawaii track meet, moved to San Francisco to set up a medical practice in the Castro District, and joined a gay bowling league. This gave him the idea to set up the Gay Games to raise awareness and fight against negative stereotypes.

called "home." Each of the lesbian bars would always have their customers who would refer to their bar. They would say, "I'm from Peg's." "I'm from Maud's." "I'm from Scott's Pit." Then there were the various gay and lesbian sports leagues. There was the San Francisco Women's Softball League. The San Francisco Bowling League. The San Francisco Pool League. All of which helped lay down the foundation for the inaugural San Francisco Gay Games in 1982, founded by Tom Waddell, with Rikki offering to help with their launch, including outreach to the lesbian community.

ALCOHOL IN THE COMMUNITY

As a customer and as a bartender, the thing that I realized was how alcohol was impacting and in some cases destroying people's lives. It almost destroyed mine. I'll be honest about it. One of the primary reasons that I left San Francisco was because of alcohol. My main places of employment were the two bars, Maud's and Amelia's. And at that time, the only places where gays and lesbians could socialize were the bars. And for lesbians, with the exception of the women's bookstores and coffeehouses, there were few other places to socialize and hang out. That dramatically changed when the San Francisco Women's Building opened. So I think a price of our gay and lesbian movement at the time in terms of the limited places we had to go and a subsequent consequence was alcohol. But now there are so many other options where our LGBTQ community and people can meet and socialize. Which might explain why there are no lesbian-owned bars in San Francisco right now.

BEING OUT IN THE ANTIWAR MOVEMENT

At the WRL–West office in San Francisco I was as out as I could be. One of the places where being gay intersected with other movements was the Vietnam War. How many lesbians and gay men were in the military? And if you remember, back then you couldn't be out in the military. That's when I realized, we had Leonard Matlovich, who got discharged for loving a man and Margarethe Cammermeyer, who got discharged for loving a woman.

Sergeant Leonard Matlovich, a gay man, was featured on the cover of *Time Magazine* on September 8, 1975, with the headline "'I Am a Homosexual': The Gay Drive for Acceptance." He had served three tours in Vietnam, earning two Air Force Commendation Medals, a Bronze Star, and a Purple Heart, and gone on to teach race relations for the Air Force. In 1974, he volunteered to serve as a test case through whom the ACLU could challenge the ban on gay servicemembers, and in March 1975 he became the first gay service member to purposely out himself.

In 1989, Colonel Margarethe Cammermeyer, chief nurse of the State of Washington National Guard and author of numerous scholarly research studies on military nursing concerns, disclosed during a routine security clearance that she was a lesbian. The National Guard discharged her in 1992, and she filed a lawsuit against the decision. In 1994, the U.S. District Court for the Western District of Washington ruled that both her discharge and the ban on gay people and lesbians serving in the U.S. armed forces were unconstitutional. She returned to the National Guard as an openly lesbian officer and served until she retired in 1997.

I'm going to jump a little forward and talk about the race issue. I was just sitting here pondering something. When we talk about marriage, it was people of color who had to deal with that issue before our gay and lesbian community. *Loving v. the State of Virginia* happened in 1967. So when the issue of same-gender marriage became a major focus of our movement, I was in support of calling it marriage equality and not gay marriage. To acknowledge that it was women, based on gender, who didn't have full equality in marriage. And that it was people of color, based on race and ethnicity, who also didn't have full equality in marriage. The faces and voices of who the public saw on this issue were white. The same was true when our gay and lesbian movement was focused on gays

Mildred Jeter, a Black woman, and Richard Loving, a white man, were married in 1958 in Washington, D.C., because interracial marriage was illegal in the state of Virginia. Five weeks after they returned home, they were arrested and a Virginia judge ordered them to leave the state. With the help of the ACLU, they challenged the law in a case that eventually reached the Supreme Court, and in 1967, the Court struck down all laws against interracial marriage as unconstitutional. The decision was a landmark for civil rights.

in the military with Don't Ask, Don't Tell. All I ask is that we do not forget those who came before us, because women and people of color have always been at the forefront.

THE MEANING OF "COMING OUT"

When I first heard someone ask me, "When did you first come out?" I would assume they were asking when was the first time I ever slept with a woman. But then, the more I thought about it, I realized that coming out was less about any sexual interaction. For me it was about coming out first to myself and owning and claiming with pride that I am a lesbian. So now I look at that question of "When did you come out?" much differently. And as an out Black lesbian, I think that for us who can be out, it is essential. Because we get to be the faces and voices of those who for whatever reasons can't be out. It is why the holding of Black LGBTQ Pride events is absolutely essential. It is why having LGBTQ-and-allies student centers in our historically Black colleges and universities is essential.

OLD AND YOUNG IN COALITION

I am part of the 47 million post–World War II baby boomers who were born between 1946 and 1964. For those who are eighteen to thirty-four years old there are 47.5 million people. If ever there was a moment to be in partnership

Mandy was a national co-chair of Obama LGBT Pride during the 2008 presidential campaign. Courtesy of The White House

and to be in movement organizing together, it is now. This country's demographics are going through the roof. Women are the numerical majority. By 2050, if not sooner, this country will be majority people of color. Keeping in mind, of course, who was already here, indigenous to these lands before any ships pulled up to these shores. I do want to know, generationally, how we can be in the same conversations. In our lifetime, we saw Obama, a Black man who's the son of an interracial marriage, become president of this country. This is extraordinary. And I think it only gets better here in the South where I live. I ain't moving! I love Durham, North Carolina! I love the

South! It is such an amazing place to live—that does have its challenges. But what better place to be?

RACISM HAS RUN OUT OF HISTORY

One of the proudest moments of my organizing in North Carolina was supporting Harvey Gantt, the first Black mayor of Charlotte, North Carolina, when he ran [*for the Senate*] against Jesse Helms in 1990 and 1996. Recently I got to see Harvey for the first time in twenty-five years, when we were both at a speaking event at Western Carolina University. He shared something with me that I'll share with you.

When a lot of Black students were integrating campuses in the South, he and his wife were students wanting to integrate Clemson University in South Carolina. They were called into the office of Fritz Hollings, the president of Clemson. He said, "You need to know that even though there are a lot of people who don't want you to integrate this campus, there's really not much that we can do about it. Because not only have we run out of time, we have run out of history." When Harvey said that to me I almost burst into tears. Because I do believe that this is where we are right now. I think a lot of the craziness is a lot of people trying to hang on to, really, what I call a white minority now. They are trying to hold back what is inevitable. So to be a part of that then, to be a part of what could be in the future, I think it's amazing. I do believe that we are in a moment. And a moment I want to be a part of. So when I look back at the Harvey Gantt campaigns, I see that in the long run he did win, because Helms has come and gone.

THE UNIFYING THREAD

In 2018, I turned seventy. As I look over these past years, I realize that a constant thread for me is realizing the importance of being humble, dreaming big, and taking risks. It's what has gotten me through my first seventy years.

CHAPTER FOUR

A Life in Leather

Hardy Haberman,
born in Dallas in 1950

Courtesy of Louis Shackleton

Hardy Haberman is tall and well-spoken. When I first met him, I was impressed by his confident physical presence and self-assurance. He grew up in a scientific home; his father was the head of the International Society of Hematology, and his mother was his father's private secretary. As a young child he spent many hours in his dad's lab, playing with slides and microscopes. He is a longtime political activist, filmmaker, and author, with a keen eye for the politics of sexuality in our lives.

In 1972 he took part in Dallas's first Pride event, and in the 1980 Pride Week he co-produced the city's first Cedar

Springs Carnival. He is well known as an educator in the leather community; he has been a guest speaker in college courses on the history of sexuality and taught classes at events such as Texas Leather Pride in Austin, Sin in the City in Las Vegas, Southeast Leatherfest in Atlanta, and Kinky Kollege in Chicago, as well as leading discussion groups in many places in the U.S. and Canada. For this work, he was awarded the National Leather Association International's Man of the Year Award in 1999 and its Lifetime Achievement Award in 2007. He also garnered the National Gay and Lesbian Task Force's Leather Leadership Award in 2009 and the Pantheon of Leather's President's Award in 2001.

Hardy has written five books and has made a number of films. Leather *(1996) and* Out of the Darkness: The Reality of SM *(2001) depict aspects of kink culture; he has also made two lesbian adult films and a documentary on the Texas state fair. His films have won numerous awards and have been screened in festivals around the world. He is currently co-chair of the board of directors of the Woodhull Freedom Foundation (also known as the Woodhull Sexual Freedom Alliance) and an active member of the Cathedral of Hope Church in Dallas, one of the largest LGBTQ congregations in the world.*

For the past twenty-two years, he has been in a relationship with Patrick Ryan, whom he calls his "boy." He also has a great sense of irony. When I interviewed him in his hometown of Dallas, he called himself a mid-century modern, and we both laughed. Asked what influenced him, he identified his parents, the gay rights movement, and the fight for civil rights. He sees his life as a series of keyframes; in filmmaking, a keyframe is an image that defines the start or end of a transition. In fact, the autobiography he is working on will be titled "Keyframes." I asked him where he was on the night of June 28, 1969, and he took it from there.

In 1969, I was probably back in Dallas. I had been going to college at Baylor University in Waco, but in counseling they told me, "Maybe you'd be happier at another school." I now look back and think, "That was great advice!" I was back in Dallas, but I didn't see anything on the news about Stonewall. The following morning, I was watching the *Today Show*. Frank Blair was on—he was the news guy—and somebody ran into the studio screaming about "Gay Power!" He tried to get the mic away from Frank Blair and Blair apologized, and then they reported about what was going on that weekend.

"HOMOSEXUALITY IN AMERICA"

In the 1960s, I was out, but I was in, you know? People come out, and then they go back in. I never hid my sexuality; I was just questioning it a lot. In high school, I had dated girls, but all my close friends were guys, and I had a lot of sexual experiences with guys. When I was eighteen I came out to my mom. After she stopped crying and saying, "Oh, I'll never have grandchildren," she started trying to set me up with guys. And I said, "No, don't do that!"

So I was just low-key. Stonewall didn't affect me as much as the 1964 *Life Magazine* issue on the homosexuals. I was on an airplane going to Paris with my family. So I'm reading this *Life Magazine*, and I see this centerfold with the bar in there, and there's, you know, the Tool Box. And I'm getting excited, you know. And there was something in there, that . . . I wanted whatever that was! I didn't read much, but I just kept looking at the picture. Looking back, it's not that sexy a picture, but I did find that . . . I don't know if it had a direct effect, but right after that, I started getting more involved.

Image from *Life Magazine* article, "Homosexuality in America," 1964.
Photograph by Bill Eppridge, © Estate of Bill Eppridge. All rights reserved.

My dad died when I was eighteen, before I went to college. My mom was kind of bouncing around for a while because she and he had been very, very close. She was very much a frustrated hippie; her motto was, "If it feels good, do it." I started playing soul music, and she was into that. She liked Jimi Hendrix; she was really an interesting person.

SEXUALITY IN COLLEGE

College was a difficult time. It was the first time I'd lived away from home. My roommate didn't show up, so I had a single dorm room; it was just me. People figured out I was gay. I didn't announce it, but they figured it out. And they figured out I was liberal. They had a group down there called the Young Americans for Freedom, which is basically the junior John Birch Society. They had me on their enemy list, because I was a philosophy major and because I went to antiwar marches, and because I hung out at the Catholic Student Union, which was where all the liberals hung out.

I've never struggled with my sexuality. Well, I struggled with it when I was in college a little bit, when I came out to my counselor, and that's when he told me I'd probably be happier at another school. I had two strikes against me. I was the Jew at Baylor. *The* Jew, the only one. Baylor is a Baptist school and has a big theology department and I was taking philosophy at the time. Big project: "Let's go witness to the Jew." It is a miracle that I ever converted to Christianity after being witnessed to on a regular basis by second- and third-year theology students.

What's funny is that one of my close friends was in the ROTC, and he's a guy who taught me how to polish boots. We'd sit up in the dorm rooms and talk and polish boots. That's how I got a really big fetish for boots.

I used to play Radio Cuba on my radio just to fuck with people. I remember vividly, someone who I thought was my friend, although I didn't know him well, came into my dorm room and started teasing me, bullying me, and ended up trying to rape me while calling me names. I had sort of blocked all that out. Then it came to me, *Wow, maybe that's why I'm so interested in trying to prevent sexual abuse!* So I wrote about it in the article in the *Dallas Voice.* I outed myself as a rape victim in the article because I think it's important. You're only as sick as your secrets, and I don't think it's a good thing to hide them. I have this weird philosophy that you're supposed to walk the walk, so I try to do it.

I got involved with the *Out of the Darkness* film because of the difference between SM [*sadomasochism as a consensual kink practice*] and abuse. And there is a big difference. When you're in the scene, you know they don't bear a resemblance to one another. Even though on the surface there is something physically potentially violent going on, it's not the same thing. Context is everything. I've always been interested in that. I've known people who have been abused. The woman I used to live with, her sister lived in Dallas, one floor down from us in the apartment building. She was raped. Some guy broke into the apartment, raped her, and jumped out the window. So I got some insight into that by being close to her, and knowing what was going on. I didn't even think about me, but maybe that's why I empathized.

SUNDANCE KIDS AND LEATHER, BUT NO MARTINIS

Around the time of Stonewall, I began getting active in the gay rights movement because it struck a chord. The movement was very active. I joined a group called the Dallas Gay Political Caucus (DGPC) in the late 1960s, the city's first gay rights group. We held our first—not a parade—it was a march. Fists in the air, march downtown. It needs to be that again.

When I was around twenty-one, I met some guys in that movement who were very masculine. I had thought to be gay you had to be androgynous, but that never worked for me. I met these guys who were very masculine— hyper-masculine, in fact. Some of them wore motorcycle jackets occasionally, and they didn't look like the quintessential leather men or anything. I asked them, "Where do you hang out? I don't see you at the bars." They said, "We go to Sundance Kids." I asked some other people about Sundance Kids and they said, "No, don't go there, that's dangerous!" So I went.

I knew that I needed to fit in because they had a dress code. They had a guy at the door. You didn't look right, you didn't get in. I went to the Army-Navy store and I got me a leather jacket, and sat in the parking lot for weeks, just looking at the door, like, "I'm going to go in," and eventually I got the nerve to go in. They didn't say anything at the door, and I walked up to the bar, and I said, "I'll have a martini, up." The bartender looked at me, and he said, "Nah, you want a beer." And I said, "No, no, no. Martini up." He said, "No, trust me. You want a beer." I got a bottle of beer, a long-neck. I stood over by the wall. I just looked and watched. I'm shy. And I realized that he did me a favor. If I had had a martini, I would have never fit in, and he could tell that I wanted to fit in. So I kept going back, and I just kept sipping beer and watching, and eventually people would talk to me. I went to the little leather shop downstairs and I got some accoutrements. Eventually I got into more of it, but I never really got into any real SM at that time; it was just sort of masculine guys having rough kinds of sex. I didn't have that much sex because I was really shy.

It's funny because before that I'd only ever had sex, I mean, honest-to-God sex, with a woman, only once, when I was seventeen. And then when I was twenty, I had a seizure. They had me in the hospital for the seizure. They figured it out and they gave me the medication and I was fine. And then they said, "Oh, by the way, you've got syphilis," and I said, "What?" I had only had sex once! So my mom was giving me shots of penicillin in the ass, and I got over it. But it was the first time I had sex and I got syphilis, so, you know, I drew the wild card and it made me a little gun-shy.

JOINING THE COMMUNITY

The reason I gravitated towards leather was because of the masculinity. You know, when my mom found out I was gay, she tried to set me up. The people she was trying to set me up with were drag queens, or they were hairdressers. I was like, "Don't do this! This is not the type of men that I like." She was like, "Well, what type of men do you like?" "The kind of men you like!" We never really talked that much about that, but I just told her, "Don't do this. Don't set me up any more."

People ask me about the leather community—where did it come from? How did it happen? It started with motorcycle gangs and coming back from the war. You know, guys like to be with guys, that whole ethos. Gayle Rubin talks about it much more eloquently than me, but I think it really was just a bunch of guys that hung around and danced—subcultures—but it became a community when AIDS hit. A lot of it had to do with the fact that these were guys that were not going to give up their sexuality

Gayle Rubin is a sex-positive feminist activist and theorist of sex and gender politics who is well respected in the leather and kink communities. She helped found a chapter of the Radicalesbians in 1971, and in 1978 she was one of the founders of Samois, the first known lesbian SM group. Among her many influential writings are "The Traffic in Women: Notes on the 'Political Economy' of Sex" (1975) and "Thinking Sex: Notes for a Radical Theory of the Politics of Sexuality" (1984). She earned her PhD in 1994 with a dissertation titled "The Valley of the Kings: Leathermen in San Francisco, 1960–1990."

and what they did. They would find safe ways to do it. We started educating people, and then it became this community, and it really bonded together. We took care of each other; we took care of guys.

Once I got involved in the Dallas Gay Political Caucus, I got exposed to a lot of the real community and a lot of them were lesbians. I did a lot of work with them. One of them ran a computer dating service, and she introduced me to a guy who ended up becoming my first boy, my first partner. My involvement in activism is what got me into activism. I was never the A-list activist; I was always the B-list.

My first relationship that I had with a guy was a daddy-boy relationship, and it ended up becoming craziness because he was an alcoholic and an addict, and I was in Al-Anon. Great partner! I should've known that the relationship was not destined to work, when the first time we get together he's shooting up. And I go, "Eh, whatever you do is . . . you know . . ." But we got together in a leather relationship. We moved out to the suburbs and got a house, and bought a dog, and did the whole thing. I lost touch with a lot of people. It may have saved my life, because we were not . . . you know, we were mutually exclusive, or at least I thought we were. Most of the people I lost touch with became HIV-positive, developed AIDS, and died. The leather community got hit really hard in Dallas like it did in San Francisco, kind of like a first wave.

After we split up, I came back to the scene. A lot of people were gone. I kept up with a couple of good friends, Frank and Carmen. Frank died. I didn't know it was HIV, I thought it was cancer. I mean, he was older. Carmen was a good buddy. He and I had played a lot, and we worked together. And he was a producer for the United Negro College Fund, for their telethon. I worked with him on that and we tried to bring it here to Dallas. We put together a whole package and we got the mayor and everybody involved, and I worked with him on that a few times. I produced a couple of shows with him. He was HIV-positive. Then I lost touch with him, and when I finally got in touch with him, he was in the hospital. When

I went to visit him, he looked like a shadow. He was always this big guy. Now he was this little skinny guy. He looked like a child. Luckily, I managed to see him before he died, but it was hard times. AIDS is still hard.

That's when I really got close to my leather dyke friends. I went to visit a friend in the hospital, Tony, the first time he was hospitalized. The nurses weren't changing his sheets. They had the infectious disease symbol on the door, and they wouldn't go in. A couple of lesbian friends would come in and change the sheets and clean him up and take care of him. The nursing staff wouldn't do it, because they were that ignorant. Even then we knew it took more than casual exposure. That was a bonding experience. Not the greatest way to bond, but it was. Through adversity.

CIVIL RIGHTS, A RABBI, AND TARZAN

My activism came from watching the civil rights movement in the 1960s, seeing the injustice there. When I first came out into the gay community, it was just post-Stonewall, barely, and the first gay bar I used to go to, before I discovered the Sundance Kids leather bar, was the Bayou Club. It was in an old antebellum house over off Hall Street. It was a dance club. They'd do barbecues and whatever on Sunday, so you'd go there and you'd dance. But they had a light that came on [if the police were coming in], so that if you were dancing with a guy, you had to find a woman, and if you were [a woman] dancing with a woman, you had to find a guy. You had to find an opposite-sex partner. They would get raided all the time. The lights would flash, flash, flash, and all of a sudden, everybody is "Hi, how are you? Nice to meet you." And if you weren't wearing at least three articles of male clothing or gendered clothing [you could be arrested for crossdressing]. I mean, there were all these weird little annoyance rules. And they would regularly come through and bust people.

So I didn't like that either! And I knew that the police didn't raid certain clubs. And why didn't they raid certain clubs? Hmm, I know why, they got money! And the Mafia ran a lot of these bars, and until recently, organized crime has been involved in it. Last twenty years or so. I look back on the Compton's Cafeteria riots in California in 1966. Different dynamic, but everything was bubbling at that time.

In the 1960s, the music of the time . . . "Something's happening here . . ." It was in the air and it was bound to happen. The first woman that I had sex with was a hippie. A genuine, dyed-in-the-wool hippie, the one I caught syphilis from. But she was a friend of mine, and that's who I'd hang out with, and we'd smoke marijuana, and that was the time! It felt liberating.

Growing up, I had a rabbi who was great. He marched in Selma and met with Dr. King. His name was Levi Olan. He's got a great book called *Maturity in an Immature*

World. Worth a read. And he used to do regular sermons on one of the radio stations here. He was a Reform Jew; he wasn't Orthodox. So his sermons were secular more than anything. He was against the war in Vietnam. He was really a firebrand. He pissed everybody off. So we'd go to Friday night services, and he'd give these sermons, and then we'd go out to dinner after. And oh, the talk was great! That's really where I got my liberalism.

And then, sexually . . . Boy, I sure did like Tarzan! I had a crush on Johnny Weissmuller, and on Buster Crabbe. There was a show, it was called *Captain Gallant of the Foreign Legion*. I don't know if you've ever seen Buster Crabbe. He was a good-looking guy. I just loved watching that show, and the gladiator movies. I loved the gladiator movies. And I thought, why do I like this?

ACT UP

I knew some people in ACT UP. They would go down to the plaza in front of City Hall at night and trace off figures. And they did it fast. Then in the morning there were all these chalk figures, like a crime scene. They did that kind of stuff. They'd chain themselves to monuments and stuff. And then we—I say we, I barely participated— but there was a big vacant lot just adjacent to the gay neighborhood that was going to be developed into a high rise, but it never happened. It was a big pit and it just sat there. One night the ACT UP guys got crosses with the

names of people who had died and made it into a cemetery. Next morning, you wake up, and it looks like Arling-
ton National Cemetery, except there were these little
makeshift crosses, and no one would touch it. The police
wouldn't touch it, the landlord, nobody would touch it. It
sat that way for months, and it made a great statement.

AIDS Coalition To Unleash Power began at the
height of the AIDS crisis in March 1987. Larry
Kramer was asked to speak at the New York
City Lesbian and Gay Community Services
Center and asked the audience if they wanted
to start a new organization focused on political
action. Two days later, 300 people met and ACT
UP, a radical direct action group united in anger
to end the AIDS pandemic, was formed.

This is before the [NAMES Project's AIDS Memorial]
quilt. I love the quilt. I wish it were something more per-
manent, but I understand the theory behind it. You know,
the first time the quilt came to Dallas, just rows and rows
of panels, friends went down, and they were docents, and
their job was basically to help hand out Kleenex. I remember walking through.

I marched on Washington in 1979. That was the first
gay rights march on Washington. I was there with the
Dallas delegation.

AMBIDEXUAL

In high school I knew I liked guys. A friend of mine in high school, one of my best friends, and I did a lot of sexual experimentation. I also had sex with women in high school, but sex with guys was always better. It really floated my boat. By 1968 I was ready to say I was gay.

Today, I call myself queer. And I do that because, in my BDSM play, I play with men, I play with women, I play with people who are transgender. It doesn't matter to me. There's always an element of it that's erotic and it works for me! But affectionally, I'm gay. My longest affectional relationships have always been with men. My boy now, we've been together twenty-two years. This is starting our twenty-third year, and it feels like, you know, yesterday! So that's been a good relationship, and I can't imagine anybody else who'd put up with me. We complement each other. But, sexually, I don't know what you'd say! Maybe bisexual? Or queer? Ambidexual?

MAGIC TRICKS, CAMERAS, SEX

I was never really closeted. I just didn't talk about it, necessarily. I never tried to hide anything. I'd always been attracted to show biz in one way or another. And I had been an amateur magician as a kid. That was the way I got over my shyness. I was always shy, and by doing magic

The Woodhull Freedom Foundation's annual Sexual Freedom Summit brings together hundreds of activists, educators, researchers, and community leaders on an annual basis to share knowledge, gain tools, and inspire all those working against injustice and for sexual freedom.

tricks, I knew something you didn't, and that made me a little less shy. I still draw on that today, because I'm still a shy person. I mean, if it were up to me, I'd be sitting on a corner, having a cup of coffee, just watching. With the Woodhull Summit, I have to go and schmooze with people. Wears me out. Like when I do presentations, afterwards I have to go up to my hotel room and collapse because it wears me out. It's a persona.

I started doing television by accident. I had a friend who was a magician, who was working on *The Bozo Show* as the Ringmaster, Paul Osborne. He said, "Hey, why don't you come down and do funny voices!" He was a magician, too. He said, "We're gonna have a character for you to do. You be Professor Tweedyfoofer." I said, "Sure, what the hell." I always wanted to get into television and communications. So I came down and put on all this makeup and I became Professor Tweedyfoofer. Sort of a

Viennese comic. I'd do an accent and all that, and it was fun! The station said, "I tell you what. I'll hire you during the day to run camera on the stock market show. Do you know how to run a camera?" I said, "Oh, yeah. Sure." I lied! And so I learned how to run a camera and I ran the stock market show during the day. There was only one camera man for two cameras. You'd go and do one, and then you'd run over [*to the other*] and have somebody yelling in your ear all the time, running back and forth. And then in the afternoon I'd do Bozo.

That's where I met my friend Mike. He and his wife and I had this ménage à trois thing going on. It was great. It was show biz; you could do anything. Everybody slept with everybody. It was wild. Our channel coordinator on the show was a wonderful dyke named Starr Proctor. Unfortunately, she's no longer with us. Starr was crazy and rode a motorcycle and wore these carpet vests, you know, that sort of 1960s hippie stuff and bell bottoms, and she always had a cigarette holder. We got along great. She was a great talker. She talked the Dallas Zoo into giving us one of their lion cubs to raise on the show. So, because of her, I got to take a lion cub home twice a week and raise a lion cub in my house.

It never occurred to me to not be out. I had never really hidden it. Even when I had my live show company, with the same guy, Paul, when we did the March on Washington, I used our conference room for news conferences, because I was doing the press and PR for it.

BEING KINKY

The kink part of it, you know, I'm out there. If you google me, you're going to find out. My associates at work are on Facebook with me. And it all started when I wrote my first book. Janet Hardy, who was a publisher at the time, said, "Do you want to use a pen name?" And I said, "What's the advantage of a pen name?" She said, "Well, you're anonymous, but people know who you are." So I said, "Eh, it's not like I'm hiding it." And from then on, there was no hiding it. I speak occasionally at the University of Texas for their history of sexuality classes for a friend of mine. I go up there and speak about leather community and history. I started doing it about ten years ago. And the first time I did it, it was all about giving a glossary and explaining terms. The last time I was up there, they were asking questions and I didn't have to explain anything. I mean, I talked about the history and I talked about safewords. They didn't ask; they knew. So I'm very hopeful. I think there's a next generation. I don't know what it's going to be like, really, I don't. Maybe it'll have to be activism again, because it ain't changing right now. I work with people that know I'm kinky. And the only question I've gotten is "So, are there any events coming up?"

Most of my film life has been kink and BDSM. Only two films are still around, and one of them is *Leather*, which is a short I did for the Dallas Film Festival, and

Cast and crew of Hardy's 1996 film *Leather*. Photo by John Noeding. Courtesy of Hardy Haberman.

that still is online and still gets comments, and Frameline distributes that. And I did one called *Out of the Darkness*, which was the reality behind BDSM. The idea behind that was as a teaching tool. Health professionals, legal professionals, and other people just don't understand it.

They need to know more about it. If you're a counselor, and a woman comes in, and she's got marks on her back, but they're nicely placed in a hatch pattern, that's not abuse. That's something she's probably pretty proud of! Even if there are marks on her neck, you need to go beyond asking, "How did that happen?" She'll tell you, it's probably not abuse, or he'll tell you. So I've done work in that respect.

I shot and co-directed lesbian porn. One was called *Gallery Erotica* and the other was called *Home Cooking*. *Home Cooking* was about this woman who ran a crunchy-granola restaurant and she falls in love with another woman. It was a romantic comedy. I learned what real lesbian sex was, not what Hollywood porn lesbian sex was, which was one reason we were so well received, and another reason we didn't make any money!

SEX AS AN OLDER MAN

I'm old, and I still have sex. Yes, I still have sex and I don't plan on stopping soon. I had a heart event last year, and they were putting me on blood pressure medicine, and I was like, "That fucks up people's sex drive, doesn't it?" No, it doesn't.

I'm still active, I'm still as horny as I was when I was a teenager. Well, not quite that, but I didn't know what to do with it then, and I know now. One of the great things about being in the leather community is, and one of my friends told me this when I first got into it, he said, "Hey, trust me. When you get older, you'll still look good in leather." For some reason, there are people that find it more attractive, and they go, "Oh, daddies!" And you know, I'm not going to be your daddy, but you could consider me that. They're attracted to that!

There's a certain admiration for experience and knowledge, and that comes with age. The "old guard" mythos. Whoever taught you, that was the old guard. There are some traditions and stuff that I was raised with—that I learned, I wasn't raised with them, but I learned. A lot of it has to do with respect and, basically, Miss Manners. If you read Miss Manners, you could be in the leather community! You don't touch that that isn't yours, you call people by whatever they want to be called, you're polite, you suit up, you show up. It's pretty simple stuff!

As I get older, I find that just as many people are just as interested in me sexually, which amazes me because I certainly am no specimen and I've certainly let myself go. I've always had body image problems. I know guys that enter a contest called Mr. Prime Choice, which is for older guys, older men in the leather community, and they'll get up there in a jock strap and let their belly hang out there, and they don't care. I think it's terrific. It's shooting the finger at the whole "body image" idea, the idea of the ideal body. I know a lot of guys who are buff, who look really good, and I know a lot of people in the porn business who are absolutely gorgeous. Some of them are in their fifties, and they're still getting work! Because there's a whole genre of people that want daddy porn. More power to them, you know? I love it!

There are challenges, you know, as you get older, but Patrick and I still have an active sex life. It's specific to what we do, you know? What we do is what we do. We don't play as much as we get older. He was never a heavy player, heavy BDSM, which is fine, you know. I accept that, that's cool; I can get that elsewhere. But we still get along great. And when I go to events and stuff, there's a lot of interest! [*laughs*] I probably am not any less active today than I used to be.

Sex with Patrick is good! Well, it's not as exciting as it was twenty years ago, but we were both thinner then! [*laughs*] We were both more agile then, but it's still good, and it's still fun, and it's still hot, and it still has its moments, and it's still intense, and that's good. It's kinky. It has to do with boots. There are always boots involved, because he has an incredible boot fetish and I do too, and so that works out. Our house looks like a *Hoarders* show for boots. There must be a hundred and fifty pair of boots, cowboy boots, in the house.

BEING A LEADER IN THE SEXUAL FREEDOM MOVEMENT

It's fun. It's exhausting. I sometimes feel I don't know what I'm doing. The mission of Woodhull is something that's important to me. The idea of sexual freedom is always something that's been important to me, because I'm a child of the 1960s. That's part of it, but I also think it's not just a fundamental human right, it's a foundation of humanity. We're all based on that. I mean, it's where it all starts, right? We're reproductive, whatever, even if you're not procreating, it's still one of the foundational drives! And the fact that in this country we cannot talk about it without tittering or making a joke or being embarrassed, or just not talking about it, is a sign of deep-seated pathology in the American psyche. That's why I work at Woodhull, because I think we need to change that.

And now more than ever! We're at a tipping point, and of course, on this tipping point, there are always people that try to pull you back. I don't think they have the strength. It's just annoying as hell. They're going to yell and scream, but they're going to eventually come along.

RESILIENCE AND WRITING

Writing is the way I maintain my sanity. I learned to start doing it. I was never an author. I learned to write scripts for TV shows and commercials. When I really started writing, when I hit my stride, was when I was writing in my journal. Journaling and doing my fourth step for Al-Anon, I tried to find a voice, and I found a voice!

It's a lot more trouble to keep up a facade than it is to just be you. It's a lot more trouble to keep a stiff upper lip than it is to just break down. I'm guilty of keeping a stiff upper lip, but also sometimes I just turn into a puddle.

I don't like the idea of people imposing themselves on somebody else. I don't like bullies. I was always bullied in school. I was a fat kid. A fat kid with glasses. The bullying wasn't bad, but it was just enough to be annoying. I didn't turn it inward, which was good. I just became a magician, which is weird, but I retreated into that. It gave me something to do. And so I've always felt that there are people that can't be out, so maybe I have to be out for them. My dad and my mom, my dad especially, used to say, "You've got to be an example." He never told me what or why, but as I've grown up, I've thought, well, maybe that's the truth, because everybody's an example for somebody else. The way you live your life is an example for somebody else. I got into recovery, in Al-Anon, later on, in Alcoholics Anonymous. You don't attract people by advertising, you attract people by living, in a program. Then they see it and they say, *Oh, I want what you have.* So that's where the resilience comes from. I've attended a lot of protests, a lot of marches. I was never hit by water cannons, never chased or anything like that. It just felt like the right thing to do. My dad wasn't necessarily a liberal, but he was a smart guy and he was empathetic and did a lot of work. He willed his library and all his papers to a historically Black college he used to work with on a regular basis. It was just the right thing to do. It felt right to him; that's what he did. When I was a kid, we'd have visitors from

India and Taiwan. They'd stay with us, because that's what you did at the time. It gave me a good ground to understand that there's a lot of diversity in this world. That gave me some resilience too.

WORDS OF WISDOM

Words of wisdom? Oh, jeez . . . "Always take a good physic every day! Have a good movement." I think the most important thing I've learned is to not take yourself so goddamn seriously. It's hard to do. For example, this mess here on my face, when I bashed my face. I fell out of bed, right? It was early morning. I was reaching over to get my watch, to see what time it was. We have a high bed, and I was reaching over, and I just went, whap! I wasn't knocked out, but I was in pain. When I looked, Patrick said, "Oh, you're going to have a shiner." My vanity kicked in and I went in the bathroom and looked at my face, and I was like [*groans*], "Jane's going be interviewing me in three or four days and what the hell, what am I going to do?" Then I realized, "It's your vanity kicking in," but it affected me. So then I said, "OK, I cannot let it affect me this seriously." So I published a picture of it online. I put it online.

The first person who contacted me was my friend Reggie Bibbs; he's out of Houston. He has a disease, neurofibromatosis. One half of his face is profoundly mutated. He speaks all over the place, and he travels all over the place, educating people about this disease. And he was the first person that contacted me and said, "I hope you're OK." And I thought, boy, if there were ever a smack in the head! It was so profound. It was like, "Holy shit, of course he'd be the first one!" We don't even talk that much and he's the first person who contacts me. If there were ever a God moment, where God is like, "Hello? Taking yourself too seriously?" And so, when Reggie contacted me, it was like, "OK! Get your ass up! Get on with it!"

So don't take yourself too seriously. And the second thing is, just do it. Just get out there and fucking do it, you know? Because if you sit around and just keep getting ready to do it, you'll never get there! Just go do it, you know? It's gotten me in a lot of trouble, and it's also been a big success.

Patrick and I have always based our relationship on a trust factor, and on a reality factor, you know? We don't put a lot of expectations on each other. Neither of us can do 24/7, as everybody seems to be doing now, because we know that's not real. So he's my boy when we're playing. In the dungeon or the bedroom, he's my boy. He calls me Sir. In regular life, we're just a couple of guys. That works for us. He knew that I did BDSM presentations, and we got together. I told him, "You know, when I go out, I play with a lot of people, I'm doing all this stuff." He said, "Yeah, I know. I know." But I'm not going to go home with anybody. He still makes me smile.

CHAPTER FIVE

Sex at a Later Age

Edie Daly and Jackie Mirkin

Courtesy of Shana Sureck

On a sunny December morning in Gulfport, Florida, just south of Tampa, I sat at the dining room table with Edie Daly and Jackie Mirkin in their lovely apartment overlooking the water on both sides. Their warmth and hospitality were complemented by the beautiful view of the bay outside and the original artwork hanging inside. This is their winter home; in the summer months, they come north to beat the heat and are part of a community of older lesbians in Northampton, Massachusetts, which is where photographer Shana Sureck shot their portrait.

Edie and Jackie have been activists for many of their later years. They met in their sixties, moved to Florida in 1981, and were married in 2008. They were featured in Without Apology: Old Lesbian Life Stories, *a book of interviews conducted by the Old Lesbian Oral Herstory Project. From the moment our conversation began, these two bold lesbians stole my heart.*

Edie Daly, born in St. Petersburg, Florida, in 1937

Edie was a suburban housewife and mother of three in the 1970s when she fell in love with a woman for the first time. In 1980 she marched in New York City with the Lesbian Herstory Archives together with Joan Nestle, the archives' founder, and she has been a leader in the lesbian community for many years. She plays a leadership role in Old Lesbians Organizing for Change (OLOC) in Northampton, Massachusetts; is a co-founder of the original radical feminist and lesbian St. Petersburg Salon, which met monthly from 1982 to 2007; and was one of the organizers of the more inclusive Salon that started in 2015 open to all women: trans, bi, straight, or gay. I began by asking her where she was on the night of June 28, 1969.

HIDDEN IN THE SUBURBS

When Stonewall was happening, I was no longer living in New York City. I was living in the suburbs, Yorktown Heights, a bedroom community near New York City. I was living with my husband and our three kids—and separated from all that was gay. My husband commuted to the city, but I didn't want to have my kids raised so that I had to watch them every minute. I wanted them to be able to be free. So there I was in the suburbs with my kids in 1969, and I saw on television the treatment of the folks at Stonewall. I was still very much heterosexual. I had hidden my own identity from myself and from everybody else. I had always loved women and I had crushes on girls and camp counselors, but I knew it was more than that.

How did I meet my husband? I was a new Florida high school graduate at eighteen in 1955 when I moved to New York City by myself, to make my way in the big city. I met my future husband that next summer on a moonlight cruise up the Hudson River. I was on a blind date with another fellow, and Phil was my friend's date. It was quite a romantic evening, and we sang and danced on the boat in the moonlight with the band and the water and the lights of the city passing by. What did I know of love except the romantic notions from the movies that filled teenagers' heads in the 1950s? It was late June and we were both working in Manhattan, only blocks from each other. He was in advertising and I worked as a mail girl at General Electric. He called the following day and asked me if I would like to go rowing in Central Park. We spent that day together and then the next and on July 2, on a little knoll in Central Park, he proposed and I said yes. We had known each other for only four days. He was nineteen years old, a smooth talker, a charmer like my dad. I was an innocent young girl who had dated only twice. I was smitten with his charms and I thought that this is what the American Dream was about: I was supposed to get married and have kids. Secondary education was out of the question. My crushes on women were pushed firmly away. No words to even suggest what I felt for women.

We were married April 27, 1957. I was twenty, Phil twenty-one. Our first son was born a year later, the second son fifteen months after that, and the third boy when the first was three. I had three babies in diapers by 1961. I knew that I was stuck in this abusive marriage until the youngest was out of school. So I just put one foot in front of the other—each day saying to myself, "Tomorrow will be different"—for seventeen years, trapped in the sub-urbs. I did what I was supposed to do, until 1974 when Darlene [*a pseudonym*] and I fell in love. She kissed me, and with that one kiss my whole life unraveled.

I knew, without a doubt, that this was what I had wanted all along. It felt like coming home. The church where I was married and where I attended from 1953 to 1961 was St. Ignatius, on the Upper West Side of Manhattan. It was known as the gay church at the time. It wasn't talked about then; there was just something understood. Almost every one of the men that attended and most of the folks at church, including the rector, were probably gay. They were in the arts. It was a High Episcopal church, and we all loved the pomp and ritual. Later on, I learned that my husband had had affairs with almost all of the gay men in the church. So I thought to myself, this frees me up some, and fourteen years later I fell in love with a woman. We worked in the same school system—I was the teacher's aide and she was the teacher—and of course we would have both been fired if there was anything overt between us. I fell in love with her in 1974, five years after Stonewall. And I can remember at one point, my husband calling her husband in the middle of the night and saying, "You know what, Marvin [*a pseudonym*]? My wife is having an affair with your wife!" And Marvin said, "Phil Daly, you are crazy!" and slammed down the phone. The thing I realized when I came out was that it was like coming home for me. It was indeed that place where I knew that this is who I am.

STONEWALL CREATED A POSSIBILITY

For me, Stonewall was a way of knowing that being lesbian was a possibility. Nineteen-seventy-four, when I came out, was the year that Alix Dobkin recorded "Lavender Jane Loves Women" with Kay Gardner and some of the other lesbian women folk singers. It was very affirming. I found myself and the woman that I fell in love with in those lyrics. Between Darlene and me we had two husbands and seven kids, so figuring how to be together was not an easy thing to do. After a few months I finally told my husband, "I need a divorce." And he said, "I tell you what. I'll leave and I'll be back in two months and you'll see how much you miss me." And P.S., he never came back and I never missed him!

How did Stonewall affect my life? For me, it was that recognition that there was another way of being. I was stuck in an unhappy marriage. I certainly loved having my children. And I enjoyed raising them and that part of being married. I knew when I came out that the kids were going to be a problem for our marriage. Not the only problem. He was an alcoholic and he was an abuser— verbally, sexually, and physically. And he was gay himself, I think, but he never would recognize that. When I finally came out to him, he said that it was my fault our marriage didn't work: I was a lesbian, and so he was not to blame for our divorce.

STEPPING INTO PRIDE IN 1980

Three years after I came out, I was ready—more than ready—to put my feet in the street. My lover had been raised a "red diaper" baby, so her orientation was toward political activism and, as a Jewish family, they were very active. They voted for [*Eugene*] Debs and she was very much an activist for civil rights. On the other hand, I was not. I came from the South. I was born and raised in Florida. People say, "Florida's not the south," but Florida is the south. My schools were segregated. I didn't even know or see any people of color. I was brought up totally with white privilege. And when I moved to the suburbs of New York, it was also what I call "white bread." All my neighbors were from the Bronx. They had moved out of the City to get away from integration—typical 1960s white flight.

Joan Nestle and other members of the Gay Academic Union founded the Lesbian Herstory Archives in 1975 as several women decided they needed a separate space to discuss women's issues. Two consciousness-raising groups formed, and one of them became the founding site of the Lesbian Herstory Archives. For the first fifteen years, the Archives was housed in Nestle's Manhattan apartment; today it occupies three stories of a Brooklyn townhouse. From the beginning it has been a grassroots community collective effort, staffed and managed entirely by volunteers, operating on inclusive and non-institutional principles and making its resources available without restriction to all lesbians as well as researchers. Today the Archives is the world's largest collection of material by and about lesbians and lesbian communities: books, movies, newsletters, posters, t-shirts, music, and more.

My first Gay Pride march was in New York in 1980. We marched with Joan Nestle and the women from the Lesbian Herstory Archives. We had huge and amazing pictures of all these historical women who were lesbian, including Eleanor Roosevelt. These were famous women who were not known to the world as lesbian. Here we were, marching with the big balloons and the whole thing. To me, it was such a high to be able to finally see my community—my tribe, as it were—and to be among them. What a heady thing it was, to be able to be there. I was still very much in the closet at home in the suburbs, but this was a place I could be out.

There was a woman in one of the nearby towns who hosted baseball games, and although I never played ball, we went to the ball games because that was where we could find other lesbians. Then, once when we went down to Greenwich Village to the Oscar Wilde Bookshop, we found a little flyer about a group of women who were living in a women's community called "A Woman's Place" in Athol, New York. We thought we'd take a ride up there. We went the day after Labor Day. They were cleaning up, because the season was over for them. They were all doing their jobs, and we were left in the living room kind of, like, still wondering, "Are they lesbians or are they not lesbians? What is going on here?" On the coffee table, we saw the *Lavender Jane Loves Women* album. That told us they were lesbians. Still, we lived this homophobic secret. Because we were afraid for our jobs and afraid of who we were. Politically, I think the 1977 march was when I realized that I wanted to be a political lesbian. I wanted to do everything in my power to find my people, to know that we were OK, and to let the world know who we were. I listened to Alix [*Dobkin, one of the members of the musical group Lavender Jane*], who said the

New York City Pride in 1980. Courtesy of Lesbian Herstory Archives

word *lesbian* from the stage. And she would say, "I say *lesbian* during my concerts, because when I was fifteen, I didn't hear anybody saying that word." I was beginning to incorporate those lyrics of Alix—and Margie Adam and Holly Near and Cris Williamson and Meg Christian—and they became my own words. I didn't know what to say. Because music is such a big part of my life, the music and those lyrics got into my body and my psyche and became my own words. The same as with the oppressor's words; they are no longer the oppressor's words when they come out of your own mouth. I had internalized that homophobia and I had internalized that oppression. In the same way, I began to internalize the empowerment. And so for me, the change that came by learning new ideas of women's empowerment is what got me on the road to becoming a political activist for lesbian rights.

COMING OUT

What was my social activism during the time of Stonewall? I was thirty-seven when I came out in 1974. Because I had a job in the school, and my kids were in the same school district, I was closeted and nobody ever said anything about my being lesbian. The microaggressions, as we call it now, those everyday slurs and homophobic jokes, were directed at other people or just in general. I knew to keep my mouth shut, because I knew that if I came out I was going to be the target now for that aggression and oppression.

In '81 my partner, Darlene, retired from the school system and we moved to Florida. Before we left New York, there was a large dinner dance for the retirees. Darlene and I danced together on the dance floor and people there either thought, "I knew that's what was happening" or they were totally shocked, and saying, "What, what are you doing?" We told them, "We're moving, we're leaving here. We're selling the house and moving to Florida! Goodbye!" Even though we knew there was nothing wrong with loving each other, we also knew not to venture beyond the prescribed line. I think the secrecy made her decide to take early retirement, even more than just the money. Moving away meant we would no longer have to live in the closet. We could come to Florida and start a new life. And we did.

THE WELL OF HAPPINESS

We started with the NOW [*National Organization for Women*] community. We opened a bookstore we called The Well of Happiness instead of The Well of Loneliness [*the title of Radclyffe Hall's famous 1928 lesbian novel*], which was code. The bookstore was here on Madeira Beach in Florida. We started a salon and within two months we knew 250 women. That salon went monthly for twenty-five years. That was the beginning of our really lesbian lives, and we talked about every single issue. We started it with a feminist consciousness that there would be no one leader. Everybody would be a leader. For twenty-five years we worked with consensus. It was amazing. Many times it took a long time to reach consensus. You could imagine, in a large community, there were never fewer than sixty-five women who came to the salon. Sometimes a hundred. Every single month. It was the alternative to the bars. The group decided in the third month that we would be in solidarity with our sisters who were in recovery, and that anything that was sponsored by our salon would be chem-free and alcohol-free. Every single issue that you could imagine, we talked about. We grew together as a lesbian community.

One of my keystone books was Starhawk's *Dreaming the Dark*. There is no difference between action, sex, and politics. Everything is connected; my political action comes out of my sexuality and who I am. The personal is political. That's who I am, and therefore that's who I want to be, integrating my whole life. We talk a lot about competing oppressions. Who is the most oppressed? It is a fallacy that one oppression is more "worthy" than another oppression. This is what intersectionality is about—the oppressions of race, class, gender, and sexual orientation.

Intersectionality is often used to describe a multiplicity of oppressions. Originally coined in 1989 by Kimberlé Crenshaw, a legal scholar, Crenshaw published the term in an article examining what she calls "a problematic consequence of the tendency to treat race and gender as mutually exclusive categories of experience and analysis."

If you can't bring your whole self to the table, if I can't bring my whole self to everything that I do, then there's a piece that is really missing, and it's a basic, fundamental piece. It's not just like, oh, the flowers are missing from the table. It's something intrinsically not there.

LESBIAN SEX

When Jackie and I got together in 1997 I was sixty years old. The first sexual experience that I had had with a woman was when I came out at age thirty-seven. I have had only two other lesbian lovers since that time. These women had had sex with men. My earlier lesbian sexual lovemaking was, I think, much more about penetration and had much more of what I call male energy. There is something very different with Jackie, who has never had sex with a man. There is a gentleness, a slowness, and a tenderness that was missing in all my other encounters sexually. With Jackie it is about going slow, enjoying the moment, and an ability to know our own bodies and our own sexual needs. Her fingers and her tongue know just where my erogenous zones lie. In reciprocation I learned a lot from Jackie and am able to relax and enjoy a much longer period of lovemaking. I am able to tell her what I need and where.

We'd both been through menopause. And then suddenly here we are being sexually active, with our hormones trying to rage again. The night sweats are from the body trying to make estrogen. And because, you know, our two bodies are trying to make estrogen again! And so there we were, sixty and sixty-six. I find the sex that I have with Jackie is the most satisfying of my whole life. And that is after sixty! I find that it is more about relaxation, where I can finally be myself. Where I can bring my whole self to the sexual experience. And talking about the politics of our lives, the political actions that we do together. We do sex together, we do politics together, our living is so blended together; even though our styles are very different, our core values are the same.

What I find, too, is that sex with Jackie, because she's never been with a man, is very different than sex with women who have been with men. It's just very different. I can remember the first time that we had sex together and I said, "Oh my god, I don't ever have to worry any more about having an orgasm." It was like she knew exactly what to do, and where, and when. And it was so wonderful that I could just relax and enjoy it.

I think there was also a need to be in control when I was younger. I could not relax and just let the feelings take me to a calm and unhurried place. The first time we had sex was so dramatically different, and I felt like it was as much about me and my letting go and enjoying whatever came along. So much so that I learned a different way of being in bed and our enjoying each other's bodies. I in turn became much more aware of how to pleasure Jackie. What she liked and needed. Again, going slowly and not worrying about achieving orgasm.

And the toys. We bought toys. But the toys that are most satisfying are external toys, not internal toys. There's never a day that goes by that we don't touch each other, tell each other that we love each other. We always have this thing about, "Do you know how much I love you?"

Edie at the New York City Dyke March in 1994 with Oak Wojtkowski (left) and Cybilla Hawk (right)

And the other one always answers, "No, tell me." We have to breathe up new ways to say how much we love each other. We breathe them up from somewhere deep inside ourselves.

TEACHING YOUNGER PEOPLE

One of the things that happened a couple of years ago was that the OLOC [*Old Lesbians Organizing for Change*] group in Northampton invited the Smithies [*Smith College students*] to come, and we had a wonderful group. There were twenty-five old lesbians and twenty-five young queer women. One of the things we did was two "fish-bowls." One was six old lesbians talking about what they don't want to hear from the younger generation, like "Don't call me young lady" or say, "You don't look your age!" The second group was six young lesbians, the young queer women—oh, *queer*, I should say, not *women*, because some don't want to be called women—speaking about what they don't want to hear. Things like "You have it easy."

I understand Foucault, and I understand that we really need to have no separations in who we are because of the broad gender spectrum of who "we" are. And I also understand the need for identity politics until it all changes. Both-and, not either-or. The young women from Smith were saying, "We understand about being queer, but we also want to call ourselves lesbian. And if we say we are lesbian, we are betraying the queer community. And they don't accept us. We need a place for us to be." And so when the students were able to articulate this, the professor who was in the room said, "I will find you a place. What are your needs?"

Because we always say, "Nothing about us without us!" At one of our salons in 2002, we invited a trans woman to talk with us about transgender issues. This issue actually split our community right down the middle. It was very contentious. After twenty-five years, we were no longer of the same mind. After a few more years, salon gatherings stopped. And in 2011, *Womyn's Words*, our publication, published its twenty-eighth and last issue. I think it was the final controversy.

This new sexual and gender revolution will not happen without anger. Anger directed in a positive place is always what spurs people to change. And it's often the young people who do the changing. They're going to do it very differently than we did.

Jackie Mirkin, born in Boston in 1931

On the day I interviewed them, Jackie was wearing a t-shirt with "peace" in English, Hebrew, and Arabic. This was one of her vast collection of political t-shirts, and I loved that she wore it for me. I also loved the t-shirt Jackie chose for the photo shoot with Shana, back in Northampton. With her seriousness there is also a sparkle. She was born in Boston in 1931, got her master's in social work in 1955 at Wayne State University in Detroit, and was on the faculty of the Rutgers School of Social Work. Though she'd had many relationships with women, she didn't come out of the closet until many years after Stonewall.

BURSTING OUT OF THE CLOSET IN HER FIFTIES

Here's what I think was happening in my personal life around the time of Stonewall. I'd never been married nor had children. I've never had sex with a man.

In 1969, I was in a closeted relationship with a woman. We had been together since 1960. We met when we worked in a Girl Scout Council—surprise, surprise!—in Royal Oak, Michigan, a suburb just outside of Detroit, where I went to graduate school. Then we lived together in New York and New Jersey, and I was working as a staff supervisor at a children's institution. In 1964 we were both hired as faculty at the Rutgers Graduate School of Social Work, where I remained until 1970.

The reason I say "what I *think* was happening" is that we were so closeted that I totally missed Stonewall as an event. And I actually missed the women's movement, even though some of my friends were a part of it. I was oblivious. I guess so much of my energy went into maintaining the closet that even though I was lonely and didn't know why I was lonely, it wasn't until much later, in the early 1980s, that I began to figure it out. I met a woman twenty years younger than I. She was an out lesbian who introduced me to lesbian feminist culture. It was then that I had my first deeply satisfying sexual experiences with another woman. She came a generation after me and I benefited from her sense of pride and free expression of her sexual identity. So that is why I say that I burst out of the closet in the early 1980s. I had a very messy affair with her, but the good part of that was that I discovered what it was I had been missing, not only in my sexuality but in my community. I found a lesbian therapist whose practice was with lesbian and gay clients, and with her support, I began to engage socially, professionally, and as an activist with the women's community, the lesbian community, and the LGBT community.

YOUTH AND EDUCATION

I'm from the generation where my mother caught me in the bathroom masturbating and told me if I kept doing "that" I was going to have to be put in an institution. And she really believed it.

I am a New Englander by birth. My mother was from the Boston area. My father's family was in Springfield. During the first eight years of my life, we lived in Boston, Springfield, Westfield, Northampton, and Connecticut. My parents separated when I was seven, and my mother returned with my younger sister and me to the Boston/Cambridge area. First we were on public welfare. Later my mom worked and supported us as a working single parent, which was quite unusual in those times.

I went to Girls' Latin for high school, which was good. It was good to be in an all-girls environment, particularly since I was fat and not attractive to boys. And I was still oblivious to what my sexuality was. From there I went to Suffolk University. It was just after the Korean War and the school, which had started as an evening law school with a pre-law undergraduate school, now had added a daytime liberal arts curriculum. They wanted to increase their female student body, so they gave me a scholarship, and I was the first person in my family to go to college. And again, it was wonderful because our small group of fewer than a dozen female students formed a Women's Association that provided support and friendship in an otherwise male-dominated institution.

Two professors were particularly positive influences on me throughout my college years. One, in his early thirties, was gay. He disclosed that to me after I had graduated, when he felt safe. The other, in her sixties, was unmarried, and as my own awareness developed in later years, I speculated that she probably was a lesbian. They mentored me and many other students. They held salons in their brownstones where, with borrowed classical music recordings from the public library and paintings from the Museum of Fine Arts, they served wine and we had conversation and discussion about cultural issues. There were no such extracurricular opportunities at the university itself, though many faculty members had high levels of scholarship and rich educational backgrounds. The school atmosphere was focused on working people who commuted, attended classes, and then went to their jobs. So it was an amazingly enriching educational experience, especially for someone with no previous exposure to that kind of life. Through those "salons" and the Women's Association, I found my closest friends—two gay men and a bisexual woman. This is all post-school reflection, since they were closeted and I hadn't a clue as to my own sexual identity.

ON THE OUTSIDE OF A SECRET SOCIETY

Through all of this I never recognized what my sexuality might be. After I had graduated, I continued a friendship with those professors for several years. When the male professor came out to me, he asked me how my best friend was. Here's how the conversation went:

"How is E.?"

"Oh, she's fine. She's married."

"To a man?"

"Yes."

"I always thought that you two were a couple. What happened?"

So I left Boston to go to graduate school in 1953. I got my master's in social work in Detroit at Wayne State, where I eventually discovered that one of my favorite professors was a lesbian. I found this out about two years later, when I had my first sexual experience with the woman who happened to be her "roommate." That woman and I remained lifelong friends long after the sexual part of our relationship ended. Still I couldn't find community, because nobody talked. So even though I now knew that I was a lesbian and felt that this was the best thing that had ever happened to me and was clear that I loved women, there was no one I could talk to about my sexuality. The women that I met didn't disclose their sexuality. Though I met many women socially and professionally who I later realized were lesbians, none of them ever talked about it. They were like members of a secret society and I didn't have the password. They were warm, loving, smart women whose company I fully enjoyed, but I always felt alone and outside. And I didn't know how or feel free to ask the right questions.

RACISM IGNITES HER ACTIVISM

My awareness and my activism really started in graduate school. We had a very famous research professor. As master's students, we had to write a thesis. There were four of us who took on a group project. There was a grant for it and we could get a little income. In that group we were three white women and one African American woman. We became very close, as that kind of group does. The white women were all the first in our families to go to college. The African American woman descended from a long line of teachers. We worked on the group project together and divided the work that had to be done. However, each of us had to produce a separate thesis. Mine was just passable because I was a good writer but I was not a good researcher. Our professor thought the African American woman's piece was stunning and gave her a very high grade, adding that it was an "unusually good paper for a Negro." That was the beginning of my direct social action. We went to the professor and we said, "This is wrong. She wrote a good paper. It's not wonderful even though she's Negro. She wrote a good paper." And he didn't get it. So we made an appointment with the dean, and the dean was very gracious and sat down with us and listened to everything we had to say. And when we were finished he said, "I appreciate your sincerity, everything that you are saying, but you know faculty members have academic freedom, so I cannot say anything to this professor about this." But my consciousness was raised then, and I began to engage in direct antiracist activities through my relationship with that same "Negro" woman.

Throughout my education, I was inspired by professors who taught me that as a social worker, I would be able to change the world. And I truly believed it and still do. It took me about twenty years of great effort to figure out, however, that I personally wasn't going to create global change. Rather, as Blanche Wiesen Cook has said, "Revolution is about process. It is not an event." I was saving the world. And I think I'm still saving it. And even though things are horrible in the present, this [2016] election could be the best thing that ever happened if it succeeds in pushing the revolution forward.

Once I finally came to the point where I actually came out, it felt like I was shot from a cannon. In 1987, I was working as a social worker in the public schools in New Jersey. I was in the newest high school in the state, a very modern building with a beautiful guidance suite where I had a private office. I was a member of the child study team, which evaluated kids with special needs, but I was also supposed to be available to give social work counseling to other students as well. And that's when I started to post articles about gay teens and their need for safety. It was dangerous for me as an employee in a time where there were no legal protections for LGBT people. But if I posted them on my bulletin board as a social worker, then a student could come in there and read them and it wasn't that I personally had said anything or done anything illegal. As a result, a lot of kids came to me who would not have, and a lot of teachers. But then I was called in to my supervisor's office at the Board of Education, and I was told that my assignment was going to be changed to a different building because a certain female teacher who happened to be a lesbian had been spending too much time in my office. She was in the office where she felt safe because she was referring kids to me. And I didn't have a leg to stand on. I could not say, "You can't transfer me; this is discrimination." I just said, "OK, you want me in that building, I'll go to that building."

A little later, I joined a statewide committee and I put together a directory of therapists for kids who were experiencing discomfort, concern, confusion about their sexual identity, making it clear that we didn't identify these kids as sick, but that they or their parents might need someone knowledgeable to talk to. This directory was sent to every public and parochial high school in New Jersey.

FINALLY MEETING OTHERS

Staying closeted—as I was for over thirty years—that was probably the most hurtful. And my partner and I were living very near the town where she grew up, near her large Orthodox Jewish family and community. She was, until the day she died, concerned about their reactions if they learned about her sexual identity. I believe that they had already figured it out. After twenty-two wonderful years, we painfully and awkwardly separated because I could no longer live in the closet. But it wasn't really until I retired that I came out fully and joyously.

I tried to find places to meet women of similar interests. I went to some of the women's bars in the Village, but I met only women who were there to drink. Then I learned about a woman who opened her home in Glenview, New Jersey, once a month on a Sunday afternoon, and it was an alternative to the bars. There I met women of varied ages (mostly in their thirties and forties) who were intelligent, fun, and, like me, recently out as lesbians.

As people in New York City used to say to us in New Jersey, "If we meet you and we like you, you know you're going to have to come here to hang out with us. You New Jersey women, you all come to the city. We don't need to come to you." It was such a New York–centric approach!

Through a mutual friend I met a woman who was going into the city on Friday nights to SAGE. And SAGE had two groups for women: one for women fifty and over and one for women forty and over. Some of the members were in their eighties and nineties. And that was just amazing, because you found every kind of political point of view, every kind of activism. Women who were coming out in their nineties. Women in their eighties who were still married to men and identified as lesbians and

> SAGE (originally Senior Action in a Gay Environment, now SAGE: Advocacy and Services for LGBT Elders), founded in 1978, is one of the oldest and largest non-profit organizations dedicated to the needs of older LGBTQ people.

would say, "I'm going to give you my telephone number, but if a man answers, hang up." I attended that group for three or four years and made some wonderful friends. I think that's where the joy of integrating all of me and claiming all of me was born, instead of fearing I would be institutionalized. By the way, for almost the entire time I was employed as a social worker, we were still categorized in the DSM as mentally ill.

> The *Diagnostic and Statistical Manual* of the American Psychiatric Association listed homosexuality as a mental illness until 1973. A variation, "sexual orientation disturbance," remained in until 1987.

SHE NEVER COULD PASS AS STRAIGHT

My hair wasn't as short as it is now, because it wasn't safe. But it didn't matter because I was never able to pass. I looked like somebody in drag in skirts. That's how you had to dress in that era. I could never pass. Which meant that I was always being told how to walk like a lady. I looked and walked like a dyke, and in my twenties, after getting my MSW, my doctor still told me repeatedly, "I'm going to teach you how to walk. I want you to put a book on your head and walk toward me."

STEPPING OFF THE CURB INTO PRIDE

My first gay pride march was in 1988, when I was fifty-seven. A friend of mine, a younger social worker in her forties who was also Jewish, had started going to the gay synagogue in New York and said, "I've never been to a gay pride march. Would you like to go?" And I said I would love to. So we had brunch and we went maybe about twenty blocks north of the Village and then we just walked over to Fifth Avenue. We stood on the curb and we watched and we watched, and I think we shared this feeling of "If only we could get into it, but we don't know how!" All of a sudden the big gay synagogue contingent came, and because she'd been going there, people recognized her. And at that point the march happened to take a rest stop. People came over and my friend ran out and hugged them and she said to me, "Come on, I want you to meet people." And I did, and I never went back on that curb. That was the end of the closet for me.

I was still working, and there were lesbians at work who were shocked. "You went to the march?" they said. "It was wonderful," I said. "People take newsreels of that and then they'll show it on TV and they'll see it at work and you'll lose your job!" "If it happens, it happens."

I would say that my resilience came from the love of other people who loved themselves and helped me know that it was OK to love myself.

LOVE AND SEX AND AGING

Edie was sixty and I was sixty-six when we met through
OLOC (Old Lesbians Organizing for Change). After I
met her and started falling in love, I made an acupuncture
appointment because I was having night sweats, which
had stopped years earlier. The acupuncturist was a straight
guy and was cool. When I told him about the sweats, he
laughed hysterically. He said, "You've just been telling me
that you are in love. It doesn't end. You know, it doesn't
matter that you completed menopause. When you have
those intense sexual feelings, your body responds."

The things that interest us—the cultural, political,
ideological—are the glues that bond us and are also the
aphrodisiacs. So it's exciting. And yes, our sexual life has
changed and that's a lot, because changes in our bodies
have changed what we're capable of doing. I had laparo-
scopic surgery last year to remove some hepatic cysts. I'd
been having aches, pains, weight loss, and loss of energy.
Also, our sleeping habits have changed; we no longer
sleep together all night. But we do a lot of hugging, kiss-
ing, fondling, lying together. I consider both of us to be
sexual. I've always had a broad sense of what sexuality is
about. I know that there has often been a sexual compo-
nent in my relationships with women I've never touched,
whether they acknowledge it or not. I just think it's in the
air and when the chemistry is there, it's there.

TEACHING YOUNGER PEOPLE

A quick way to teach younger people, and then I'll say a little more, is to quote Oscar Wilde, who said, "Be yourself. Everyone else is taken." I really think that's true. And I think what I have learned that has been the most valuable to me is to try to be honest about who I am and what I need. And that there is no shame in embracing my sexual identity.

People are not mind readers, and what I've seen a lot among women is that much strife that arose from the expectation that other people could read their minds could have been eliminated. "You knew I was attracted to you!" "No, I didn't." And more explicitly, when we're talking about sexuality and our sexual needs, even if you've been very active sexually and have all kinds of tricks and toys, you don't automatically know somebody else's body and what she needs. You need to listen, you need to encourage her, and you need to speak for yourself in saying what pleases you, what doesn't please you, what makes you uncomfortable. And I think that's true holistically, not just about your body.

CHAPTER SIX

Love, Loss, and Laughter

Lani Ka'ahumanu, born in Edmonton, Alberta, in 1943

Courtesy of Bruce Antink

I knew I was going to like Lani Ka'ahumanu as soon as I heard her laugh. She has a great laugh and loves to find humor in even the bleakest of stories. She identifies as bisexual or queer. Lani was conceived in Hawai'i and was born in Edmonton, Alberta, where her dad, a Marine civil engineer, was stationed during World War II, working on the Alaska Highway connecting Alaska to the rest of Canada and the U.S. She grew up in San Francisco and the Bay Area. Lani has traveled across the country as a bisexual activist, organizer, author, and safer sex educator and was the strategic political architect of the bisexual movement of the 1980s and 1990s. She co-edited the groundbreaking feminist anthology Bi Any Other Name: Bisexual People Speak Out *with Loraine Hutchins in 1991, and the two wrote a new introduction for the book's second edition, issued on its twenty-fifth anniversary in 2015.*

Lani originally came out as a lesbian, and when she began speaking out in 1976, she was embraced by the women's community, her professors, and other students in the nascent Women's Studies Department of San Francisco State University. However, in 1980, when she realized she was bisexual and came out again, she faced derision within the communities she called home. Her story reminded me once again how difficult we can be to our own. When I asked her about where she was at the time of Stonewall, I heard about young Lani beginning a lifetime of activism.

KINDERGARTEN ICE CREAM AND BLACK PANTHER BREAKFASTS

I didn't hear about Stonewall or grasp the meaning of the rebellion until several years afterwards. I graduated from high school in 1961 and married my high school sweetheart, the captain of the football team, in 1963, and by 1966 we had a son and a daughter. My husband taught at our old high school! We only went to one faculty party. It was way too weird. I was a full-time suburban housewife and mother. I remember thinking once that I'd already done everything I was supposed to do in my life.

By 1969 I was a full-blown activist with Another Mother for Peace, speaking out against the Vietnam War, ICBMs, and nukes. And standing with Cesar Chavez and the United Farm Workers grape boycott, and collecting food for the Black Panther breakfast program, because it made total sense to me. All of it did. I'd felt a connection with the Civil Rights movement since I was a kid. I grew up with black and white TV images of police dogs and fire hoses and kids my age and adults standing up for what they believed, even if it meant getting injured or worse. Their courage and commitment over the years made a lasting impression on me. The violence and government lies about the Vietnam War and the assassinations and uprisings motivated my dedication to activism and changing the world.

I'd started taking a night class each semester at the local junior college. In 1968–69 the women's movement unfurled banners at the Miss America pageant and their street theater got a lot of press, so they were on my radar. I was volunteering at my son's kindergarten class. By the time my daughter started school a couple years later I was the recess lady on Wednesdays, the ice cream lady on Fridays, and ran the art corner on Mondays.

My husband and I met a month after my sixteenth birthday. We went steady, and I married at nineteen. I was so young, but on the path that had been set out for me. It was a fairy tale life for a while, but it just wasn't my life. I tried. I did everything I could think of doing to make it work. We were sort of suburban hippies, with an organic veggie garden in the backyard. I canned all sorts of jam and pickles and was sprouting legumes, experimenting with recipes from the *New York Times Cookbook*, learning Asian cooking, sewing my children's clothes, and painting, wallpapering, and upholstering, everything you can imagine and then some. And I was pretty good at most of it; but it just wasn't me. I had fun volunteering at the school and loved working with the kids and adored my own children too, but something was missing, something was not right. Activism made me feel alive, made me part of something bigger, and it was the dawning of the Age of Aquarius and peace would rule the planet with harmony and understanding and all of us were in it together. I sincerely believed we could change the world. I still do.

The more exposure [I had] to feminists on the afternoon talk shows, the more the women's movement began to make sense to me. I changed from Mrs. to Ms.—sounds pretty silly now, but back in the mid-late 1960s in the suburbs it was bold for a married woman to do this. I knew it was sort of edgy and would reveal I was identifying as—well, I was coming out as a feminist, but didn't understand how disturbing it would be for some people. My family, especially my aunties, were horrified and shamed me, saying I embarrassed the family. When I asked my husband about it later, he said it was no big deal to him.

Between going steady and our marriage, my husband and I were together about fifteen years. We grew up together, but we grew up to be different people. We divorced in 1974. He was really my best friend. I had been crying a lot and didn't know why. I was confused, and probably depressed too. He just said, "I figured out why you're crying all the time. You need to leave; you've never had a life of your own. I'll take the kids. You can't do what you need to if they're with you." I think he didn't want to be alone either. As soon as he said it I *knew* he was right.

I jumped into my new life six weeks later. I found a studio apartment about a mile away, to stay close to the kids, and the school hired me as a teacher's aide. To this day leaving my young children with their dad is the most difficult thing I've ever done. Most especially that first year, I cried myself to sleep most every night knowing in every cell of my being I had to leave them. I never looked back once. I was in the world on my own for the first time in my life. I was in my early thirties. The last time I'd been single I was sixteen and living at home! Life was an adventure. I'd already been sitting in on some early women-focused classes at San Francisco State [*SFS*] with friends. I transferred from College of San Mateo to SFS, and that's when I started meeting lesbians, activists, out-of-the-closet dykes; woman-identified, women-loving women everywhere, all around me. I felt excited, attracted, and scared too.

I heard about Stonewall about the same time I heard about bravery and breakthroughs in San Francisco in the early 1960s. Jose Saria, a drag performer, ran for the Board of Supervisors in 1961. He was also a gay rights activist.

And the Council on Religion and the Homosexual held a conference in the mid-1960s with major religious leaders. There was a ball, and many men came in high drag. The cops arrested and jailed them. The ministers were outraged and came forward to defend them. It was all over the newspapers, and the police didn't look good. And now we know about the Compton Cafeteria riots in the Tenderloin in 1966. People were standing up; it wasn't easy by any stretch, but San Francisco's history meant a little more to me.

> In 1965, the Council on Religion and Homosexuality (CRH) held its annual fundraising ball in San Francisco and was raided by the police. CRH had been supported by most of San Francisco's more progressive clergy and the police raid resulted in a tremendous amount of bad publicity for the police. It helped create a place for gay rights on the city's progressive political agenda.

I came out as a lesbian two years after the divorce. Back then "women's" pretty much equaled "lesbian." Women's culture and music was exploding in the Bay Area. Olivia Records, Cris Williamson, Meg Christian, Linda Tillery, Teresa Trull, Sugar Mama Gwen Avery, Holly Near, and women-only concerts. There was an all-women auto repair place, and women's newspapers, and women's bookstores and women's cafes were popping up on both sides of the Bay. I was a student leader helping to form the Women's Studies Department, working with professors like Sally Gearhart and Dorothy Haecker and many others, who taught me to understand myself as a woman in the patriarchy. It seemed like there were grandstands full of lesbians cheering everyone on: "Yes! Come out!" "We're here for you!" "What are you waiting for?" And when you did come out you could almost hear the roar of the crowd!

My lesbian coming-out process felt awkward and silly and sometimes scary new. Like when my friend and I were just coming out. We sat together in her car outside our first women-only party. We were so anxious we couldn't get out of the car. After a couple hours of watching women go in or come out we began laughing, because the party was going to end before we made it inside. We finally walked in, and to my shock someone shouted, "Lani!" and it was the younger sister of someone I knew in high school. "Are you here?" And it was like, yes! Wow, here I am at a lesbian party and I know the woman giving the party! So it was like that, we were all "filling up and spilling over in an endless waterfall."

> Lani is quoting Cris Williamson's song "Waterfall," from her album *The Changer and the Changed* (Olivia Records, 1975). The album was an immediate hit and helped to launch a whole genre of women's music.

Coming out to my family, though, was very different. I grew up in a Catholic family, so in their eyes I'd already committed the biggest sin of all—leaving my children. That's worse than leaving the church, which I'd done in the Sixties. So coming out lesbian, on top of leaving my children and everything else, added another notch to my "outlaw" status. The one hilarious thing that happened, though, is when I came out to my ex-husband. He told me I was a bisexual. I told him there was no such thing!

I loved Women's Studies! Every class thrilled me, challenged me, and nurtured my sense of self in the world. It didn't matter if I didn't know a socialist feminist from a Marxist feminist, or a spiritual feminist from a cultural feminist from a radical lesbian feminist. My heart was finally home. I took it in as best I could. I loved the passionate discussions. I'd been on a business track in high school so I'd have skills in case my husband died. I didn't have the training for debate or intellectual analysis. But I did speak up when the professors or classmates talked about the women in the suburbs, the housewives, the mothers. That was me they were talking about, and I could speak to that experience rather than some academic research about us. I joined the Women's Studies Hiring Committee and supported myself working at the Pregnancy Consultation Center, doing office work, pregnancy tests, and birth control, tubal ligation, vasectomy, and abortion counseling. I began to speak out as a lesbian mother and performed with Mothertongue Feminist Reader's

Mothertongue Feminist Theater is a performance collective founded in 1976 by Lani Silver and other women at San Francisco State University, with a focus on women and violence. It was born out of the realization that it was easier to read one's stories aloud than to talk about them. Early scripts included *Breasts and Roses*, *Mothers and Daughters*, *Sex Roles*, *Women and Work*, *Women and Anger*, and *Women and Rape*.

Theater. We were in the streets celebrating the first successful gay rights ordinance put to public vote, in Dade County, Florida. When it was overturned, the news spread quickly. We took to the streets again. Harvey Milk was a rising star.

Anita Bryant's national Save Our Children campaign and the reversal of Dade County's gay rights ordinance mobilized gay people in cities across the country, including San Francisco. I marched with Harvey Milk and hundreds, maybe thousands, of other gay and lesbian people. The Briggs Initiative targeting homosexual teachers made it onto the California ballot. The statewide No on 6 campaign brought out thousands of us who went door to door, introducing ourselves and explaining what the initiative meant for us. I went to a family gathering in the suburbs with my No on 6 button pinned on me. One of my

In 1977 Anita Bryant, an arch-conservative singer, former beauty queen, and spokeswoman for the Florida Citrus Commission, led a coalition called Save Our Children in a successful fight to repeal a recently passed ordinance in Dade County, Florida, that had banned discrimination on the basis of sexual orientation. It was an early instance of organized opposition to LGBTQ rights, and it inspired similar efforts in other states. In reaction, activism surged around the country. LGBTQ people staged a national "gaycott" of Florida orange juice and protested vehemently at Bryant's appearances. Olivia Records released an album titled *Lesbian Concentrate: A Lesbianthology of Songs and Poems*, with a cover design patterned after a can of orange juice concentrate.

Proposition 6 was called the Briggs Initiative after its proposer, California state senator John Briggs. It would have banned "the advocating, soliciting, imposing, encouraging or promoting of private or public homosexual activity directed at, or likely to come to the attention of, schoolchildren and/or other employees" for teachers, counselors, and administrators throughout the California public school system. Even providing health information or mentioning that a historical figure was part of the LGBTQ community could have meant losing one's job. Its defeat was a blow to Briggs, Anita Bryant, and the Save Our Children coalition.

brothers-in-law and I had a decent conversation about it. No one else approached me or my button, but they got the message. At the time I didn't know there were bisexual and transgender activists involved too. It was an incredibly heady time. I was part of the growing gay and lesbian national consciousness, a movement for change.

> Lesbians were challenging the use of the word *gay* as an umbrella term, pushing to have the community and movement described as "lesbian and gay." Lesbian issues and concerns were often quite different from gay men's at this time; many lesbians had children and might be involved in custody battles with ex-husbands. And of course women then, as now, struggled against individual, institutional, and structural sexism, including a significant wage gap. Bi and trans people were also fighting for visibility and for wider awareness of their own struggles.

COMING OUT AS BISEXUAL

In 1979, I graduated from Women's Studies. I was sort of burned out, definitely exhausted, and needed a job. I wasn't sure what I was going to do. It's funny how it turned out, though. Cooking was one of the skills I picked up and refined as a housewife. My daughter said, "Remember the camp I went to last summer, The Village OZ?

They need a chef." And it was, get this, owned by wealthy hippies. I'd heard the money came from the family who invented the Popsicle! So I was interviewed, cooked dinner for them, and we totally hit it off. The owner says, "Oh, it'd be great to have a lesbian chef." OZ was a New Age, vegetarian, clothing-optional, back-to-the-land getaway in Northern California. There were cabins, a yurt, a barn with bunk beds, a basketball court, a library, and an all-day-stoked wood fire–heated hot tub. They hosted a family camp and a kids' drama camp, massage weekends, runners' weekends, tai chi weekends, and people just came to stay. The land was gorgeous; there was no electricity or phones or sugar. A small geodesic dome sat in the middle of the organic veggie garden where we'd go to smoke grass when guests were present. The place had a resident masseuse, a gardener, a handy guy, and me— the chef and community house manager. It was laid-back, straight, and cool. I was happy to be out of the city and relieved to be away from activism.

I arrived a week after graduating from Women's Studies and put up feminist posters all over the kitchen, located a few steps above the large dining area so it was like a stage. The biggest poster had a quote from a Judy Grahn poem: "The common woman is as common as a common loaf of bread—and will rise." As the community house manager I welcomed the guests and gave the what's-what intro talk. I was out and open, comfortable, and loved being the lesbian chef.

I had my first major mutual falling-madly-in-love relationship with a woman. Merry arrived with her family and ended up joining the OZ crew, taking care of the goats and teaching us how to make cheese and baba ganoush. Not much time passed before we were head over heels in love. I brought her out. I'd had girlfriends before, but this was head-to-toe, no-hesitation electric. We were ecstatic. The shared attraction and sexual intensity had never happened quite like that before.

Eleven years earlier, when I'd started going to night school, I promised myself that if I graduated from college I'd go live in Hawai'i for a while. I was the first in my family to graduate. At the end of the summer season I went to DC for the 1979 March on Washington for Lesbian and Gay Rights and then off to Hawai'i. Merry stayed at OZ, bolstered with all my women's music and feminist books. I lived in Maui for seven months and ended up snagging a job at the popular Aloha Cantina in downtown Lahaina. I was out of the closet there, too, and before arriving I had decided I'd tell everyone I was a writer. Everyone believed me, and so I've been one ever since! Funny.

By the time I returned for my second summer at OZ, I was missing my activist life in the city and being around feminists discussing issues. I was looking forward to moving back and jumping in. Merry had come out and moved to a place nearby with her children and lover. A young man arrived, intending to be there a couple days before heading up the coast. Bill ended up staying and assisting the gardener. Everyone, including guests, had to do karma yoga in the garden and the kitchen every day. I'd give them tasks to assist with feeding our base of fifteen up to a hundred people. Things like "Please dice five pounds of onions," or "Wash the two rows of spinach the gardener brought in," or "Grate five blocks of cheese," you get the idea.

The first time Bill was in the kitchen doing karma yoga he asked if I'd read Adrienne Rich's *Of Woman Born*. He loved the book and hadn't found anyone to talk about it with. I was surprised and curious. He wanted to talk about the institution of motherhood? As a student I had co-taught a "Radical Look at Motherhood" class and that was our text! Heck yeah, I wanted to talk! We'd have these incredible discussions. My mind was a little blown. I didn't quite grasp what was happening. Then I realized we were flirting with each other, and it went on from there quickly.

Adrienne Rich was a poet, feminist, an intellectual, and achieved a kind of icon status with lesbians for her fiercely public, political, and erotic lesbian poetry. Her collection *Twenty-One Love Poems* was published in 1976, the year she came out.

He identified as a bisexual, a community organizer, and he saw feminism as a global philosophy and healing for the world. I was completely taken by surprise. We fell in love talking about organizing a bisexual feminist revolution. We talked about community organizing and movement building and women and men working together and bisexual feminism as an inclusive unifying force. The only problem was I couldn't say I was a bisexual. I just couldn't do it. I was so biphobic; it was unthinkable and painful and overwhelming. And yet there was no getting around the profound philosophical, spiritual, political, psychic, and sexual connection we had. We also shared the same sense of humor and laughed a lot. I think that saved me. For almost a year the closest I came to identifying as bisexual was "lesbian-identified bisexual," and even that was difficult to do.

Even though it had been scary coming out as a lesbian, it felt right. For my whole life I'd had crushes on girls and then women too. Coming out lesbian made sense and was a good fit. Coming out as a bisexual was much more difficult; I didn't fit in anywhere. Bisexuality made no sense. There was no visible community, no coming-out books, no nothing to support my experience. I'd been a biphobic lesbian, so I knew what was coming my way. Bisexuals were traitors and needed to choose a side. I squirmed at the thought people would think I was into threeways and was a swinger. My own biphobia was so embedded I had a hard time taking on a bisexual identity without the "lesbian-identified" in front of it. Everything I'd ever heard about bisexuals was up in my face. I'd never heard anything positive.

In that first year I called myself a lesbian-identified bisexual, which upset many and confused others. To attach "lesbian-identified" to "bisexual" was just plain wrong but buffered my own isolation and biphobia. I wanted my community to know I was still woman-identified. Saying I was a lesbian-identified bisexual was a shortcut statement about my political and community history. I was more lesbian than heterosexual, but didn't have a clue what being a bisexual meant outside of these two options. I wanted to distance myself from bisexual stereotypes. I wasn't into threeways or a swinger. It took me quite a while to challenge all my sexual judgments, stereotypes, and misinformation to conclude there's nothing wrong with threeways or being a swinger or any sexual choices people make if it's consensual.

LEAVING OZ FOR SAN FRANCISCO

I was feeling more and more apprehensive. The summer season was coming to a close. The final workshop ended, and I was moving back to San Francisco to my women's/lesbian community. Bill hadn't seen his parents in two years and had had a month-long East Coast trip planned.

I knew I'd find out who my friends were for sure. An old friend blurted, "Oh, no; if it can happen to you it can happen to me." So? There were friends who told me they didn't or wouldn't invite me to their women-only party because "You might bring your boyfriend!" Are you kidding me? Another time a woman said, "I can only relate to your lesbian half." That cracked me up. Which half would that be? I mean, there were no Emily Post guidelines for us, but some of it was so irrational, and some of it was just plain cruel and included public humiliations.

Right after a big successful NOW pro-choice march, I was standing around with maybe ten women, talking. Irene and her popular black lab Natalie, a well-known crotch-sniffer, was there. I knew Irene from Mothertongue. She'd introduce Natalie as a lesbian and joked that Natalie only sniffed lesbian crotches. We'd always

The National Organization for Women, founded in 1966, was one of the first national feminist organizations. In its early years its relationship with lesbians and lesbianism was turbulent; NOW president Betty Friedan called lesbians a "lavender menace" and kept the Daughters of Bilitis, a lesbian group, from being listed among the sponsors of the first Congress to Unite Women in 1969. In San Francisco's Bay Area, however, lesbians felt comfortable participating in NOW events.

laugh. After the march we were in high spirits, the energy was great, and suddenly, out of the blue, Irene announced, "Natalie won't be sniffing Lani's crotch anymore." Inferring I had a tainted crotch. Irene's lover told her to stop. I was stunned. The conversation quickly shifted and I left, mortified. Friends asked if I ever had leftover sperm inside me. If they had a bisexual girlfriend how would they know? I'm not even kidding you. I mean, it was that crude and that personal. But no one could shake my truth or my place in what would become the LGBTQI community and movement. Some of our history is not pretty.

I was still in the Mothertongue Feminist Theater Collective. A substitute was needed for the *Loving Women* script. I'd performed in it before, so I volunteered, and a big hubbub erupted. Was it OK for me to perform in *Loving Women*? I was an out bisexual. I didn't *really* love women like before, so a different substitute was found. I decided Mothertongue needed to do a women and sexuality script. I put a call out in our newsletter, and a writing group formed. All Mothertongue writing is from personal experiences and performed like *The Vagina Monologues*— or maybe it's the other way around; *The Vagina Monologues* is performed like Mothertongue! We were four lesbians, a bisexual, and a heterosexual woman. We wrote *"Did you come or fake it?" Women and Sexuality*, and performed it from 1981 to 1983. It was a wild success; I loved and was supported by the women in the script. We performed at women's cafés, art and event spaces, women's music and comedy festivals, conferences, and many other places, including the Valencia Rose Cabaret, the first gay comedy club, where I was working. I wrote about many different things, including a few with a bisexual focus.

All Mothertongue performances had a Q&A and discussion afterwards. Some of our ideas for new writing would come out of these interactions. My bisexuality was always questioned. I was on the hot seat. I learned how to field questions and educate. My personal was as political as anyone else's, so I spoke from my experience and talked about my own coming-out process and biphobia and misinformation. Doing it that way, I could handle the heat of the seat! People came and thanked me afterwards, and sometimes asked if they could talk with me. My answer was always yes. I loved talking with people. It relieved my isolation and was the nitty-gritty work of community organizing.

MEETING OTHERS

In San Francisco, from 1976 to 1984, there was a Bisexual (or Bi) Center on Hayes Street near Masonic. They offered coming-out groups, parenting and support groups, and counseling services. There were social events, and every year the Bi Center had a contingent in the gay pride march. Their newsletter, *The Bi Monthly*, was mailed internationally. The founding organizers, Maggi Rubenstein and Harriet Leve, were identified with feminism

> The Bisexual Center of San Francisco was founded in 1976. In 1977, the center sponsored a press conference with lesbian activists Del Martin and Phyllis Lyon and pediatrician Dr. Benjamin Spock to protest Anita Bryant's "Save Our Children" campaign.

and the gay and lesbian community, and those who volunteered and showed up were more mainstream and straight-identified. When Bill and I heard about the Bi Center we went to check it out. It was located in the bottom flat of a two-unit building. We didn't connect with anyone then, but I spotted a notice for a bi women's coming-out group. I learned so much at the one meeting I attended. All the women were in different stages of coming out bisexual from a more heterosexual life and cultural experience. Some had ongoing crushes on women and had a little dating experience but didn't know how to approach a woman or feel comfortable asking a woman out. How to dance, who leads? How does it all work? How do you know when it's all right to kiss a woman, make the first move? Why are lesbians so angry? I could answer all their questions, but I knew no one there had experience or answers for my situation. My questions would be answered within my lesbian community.

I remained visible and active, serving on committees, producing women's dances and events, and ended up managing the Valencia Rose. Bill was at SFS majoring in

Women's Studies. We knew there were bisexuals within the gay and lesbian community and movement. The longer I was out, the more lesbians and gay men came out to me in private, passing my phone number on to people who'd call and say, "You don't know me, but . . ." I became the confessional for many lesbian and gay people, including leaders who'd say, "Well, actually I'm bisexual but I can't come out, I'd lose credibility" and then ask for advice. "You're braver than me, I can't be out" or "I have a great community job and don't want to lose it so I keep all this under wraps." I knew I wasn't alone, but the community we wanted to organize was in a deep dark closet.

Eventually Bill and I met five out bisexual feminist activists who were working within the gay and lesbian communities and movement. They were all connected with the leadership of the Bisexual Center. In March 1983 we founded BiPOL—Bisexual Politics. The first political action was an educational picket line in front of the Haitian Embassy: "Stop Arresting Gay and Bisexual Men." Haiti's tourist industry was in ruins due to racist U.S. health authorities linking AIDS to Haiti.

AIDS CHANGED EVERYTHING

The HIV/AIDS crisis took over everything. Gay and bisexual men were falling ill and dying within weeks. At first nobody knew how or why. The Castro was my neighborhood. The horror of that time is still difficult to grasp. I lived through the grief, the rage, the organizing, the weekly memorials; neighborhood friends, acquaintances, waiters, retailers disappearing, dying; and everyone checking the growing number of obituaries in the weekly *Bay Area Reporter.*

The Bi Center closed in 1984. Everyone on the Board and those of us in BiPOL were involved in different areas fighting HIV/AIDS. Bi Center attendance was down. People were fearful and stayed away from the city.

Rather than risky behavior spreading HIV, bisexual-identified men and, later, bisexual women too became an easy scapegoat, and still are in many ways. On the other

> In 1981, David Lourea began actively developing and disseminating safe sex outreach at the baths and BDSM clubs, including the Catacombs. In 1983, he was appointed to Mayor Dianne Feinstein's first AIDS Education Advisory Committee and worked for two years with the San Francisco Department of Public Health to finally have bisexual men added to their weekly AIDS morbidity and mortality report. This model was then used by public health department offices around the country. Maggi Rubenstein was an early co-chair of Mobilization Against AIDS. Autumn Courtney was involved with a research study on women and AIDS.

hand, bisexuality was considered a stage, not an orientation, so targeted prevention messages were not being developed. Bisexuals were told to pick up the gay and the heterosexually focused prevention pamphlets and just read both. Back then you'd have to go to a gay HIV/AIDS organization for their info, and then to an organization that targeted heterosexual identity for theirs.

I've been part of the women's health movement since the 1970s. In the 1980s, because of the erasure and targeting of bisexual-identified men (and, later, women), I began advocating for bisexuals within the HIV prevention and safer sex education field. This began to challenge whatever sex negativity, shame, embarrassment, judgments, misinformation, ignorance, and/or attitudes I still carried around.

BIPOL STREET THEATER

Part of what kept me going and sane in a time of so much death and despair was political theater. In 1984 Bill and I came up with an idea. San Francisco mayor Dianne Feinstein [*now a U.S. senator*] never participated in the pride parade—it was not her thing. We decided to have Mayor Bi-Anne Feinstein and Princess Bi, from England, come and join our BiPOL parade contingent. We rented a red 1972 Oldsmobile convertible, and two bi women did incredible character studies of both of them. Mayor Feinstein at the time had a big helmet hairdo and wore her signature silk blouses with a tied bow. So we had Mayor Bi-Anne with the same hair, blouse, and bow, and conservative jacket and skirt, and the very pregnant Princess Bi held a little sign pointing to her stomach saying, "Bi-Son." They sat on the back of the convertible. An Elton John impersonator drove the car, with a large banner spread across the car's front grill declaring "Mayor Bi-Anne and Princess Bi Welcome You to the San Francisco Bi Area." Bill was a giant clam, a "bi-valve for human rights"; there was a "bi-detector"; and my daughter Dannielle and her friend Ann from high school were marching as giant sandwich-board "bi-cuspid" molars, holding "We Are Everywhere" signs. We had "bi-ceps" (strong people), and I always marched as "Bi and Large." There were only maybe nine of us at first, but by the end of the parade there were twenty-seven people. We received the coveted Most Outrageous Contingent award presented by the old-school Tavern Guild, so it was really quite a deal for us to be chosen.

Also in 1984 the Democratic National Convention was held in San Francisco a couple weeks after Pride, in mid-July. In January, BiPOL secured the first permit for one of the city-provided protest stages during the convention. I ended up running for vice president of the United States. The fee and paperwork were filed. Anyone can run for vice president. You just have to get two hundred valid delegate signatures for your candidate and you qualify for fifteen minutes on the floor of the convention to nominate

Lani marching with BiPOL contingent in the 1984 Lesbian & Gay Freedom Day Parade. Courtesy of Arlene Krantz, BiPol co-founder and bisexual activist

someone. Free media time, and you can use the time any way you want. We wanted the time to talk about gay, lesbian, and bisexual families, AIDS funding, passing the ERA, and more.

We also organized the first bisexual rights rally. Three to five thousand extra media were in town covering the DNC and would arrive early for the parade festivities. They'd be looking for stories. We wanted bisexual visibility in local media, but maybe we'd score some national media too. Everyone was playing the media—The Sisters of Perpetual Indulgence planned an extravagant sexual healing of Jerry Falwell at Union Square. Jerry and the

> The Sisters of Perpetual Indulgence call themselves a "leading edge Order of queer and trans nuns" using "wit and irreverent humor" to "go forth and sin some more!" Their first appearance was on Holy Saturday in 1979, and they have since devoted themselves to "community service, ministry and outreach to those on the edges, and to promoting human rights, respect for diversity and spiritual enlightenment."

Moral Majority were also in town presenting their Brotherhood Family Forum. To kick off my run for VP we sent out a press release that BiPOL would introduce our candidate and platform at Moscone Convention Center at 1:00 P.M. The press showed up and we got a two-inch story in the *San Francisco Examiner*. Our "Tippecanoe and Ka'ahumanu Too" campaign got local and national attention. Unfortunately Mondale chose Geraldine Ferraro over me and Mayor Dianne Feinstein, who was also in the running. Bisexuals made it into a political cartoon, Herb Caen's column twice in one week, a morning talk show out of Chicago, and various newspapers. The longer, juicier stories will be in my memoir.

At the Bi Brunch Bisexual Rights rally, Mayor Bi-Anne presented me, the VP candidate, with a key to the city

I'd made out of cardboard and covered with foil. We had a pretty impressive lineup of performers and speakers, including my seventeen-year-old daughter addressing a teenager's right to sex education and access to birth control in high school. Sister Boom Boom, the Sisters of Perpetual Indulgence, the Ladies Against Women Troupe, and a Reagan impersonator who was in town performing at a club showed up and said he was bisexual and thought the rally was the coolest thing. He asked to perform and I said, "Yeah, come on up!" There were more people scheduled to come on stage than in the audience. If you were looking at the stage it was really quite impressive, with the banners and everything, but if you were on the stage looking out, there were a few clusters of people scattered about sitting on blankets, cheering wildly. Every one of us knew we were making history.

A National March for Lesbian and Gay Rights from Castro to Moscone Convention Center was happening around the same time as our Bisexual Rights Rally. BiPOL had contacted the organizers asking how we could assist with the National March, and maybe work together. We were told we weren't allowed to march. And we were like, "Are you kidding? You want us to cheer you on from the sidelines?" Yes, they said, that would be fine. Unbelievable. So someone else from BiPOL asked and got the same answer. If we were closeted bisexuals we could get away with marching, but because were out of the closet we were banned. Yes. We were appalled. I mean, really?

Really? But we already had this rally planned and were setting up a beverage booth, so we had enough to do. The National March organizers hadn't thought about providing something for people to drink after they'd marched the three miles on a sunny day. As the people poured into the demonstration area, our beverage booth sold out! This was the most successful fundraiser BiPOL had ever had, delivering a huge financial boost for our community organizing work.

LIFE CHANGES AND LESBIAN SEX CLUBS

What changed my life in the early 1990s was landing the HIV Prevention Project Coordinator position at Lyon-Martin Women's Health Services for a two-year amfAR grant targeting young high-risk lesbian and bisexual women, assessing their HIV prevention and safer sex knowledge and whether they practiced safer sex.

I hired a team of peer educators. We were lesbian and bisexual women, with women of color representing. The ten of us went through an intense HIV/STI prevention, education, and interview training. We were the Peer Safer Sex Slut Team—PSSST—to get attention and for sizzling hot. The front of our black t-shirt interview "uniform" was emblazoned with "Safer Sex Sluts Dedicated to Demolishing Denial." I developed a women's safer sex kit. It's a folded triangle, and when it's fully open there's a vulva, with two hands holding down a dental dam. I

Women's Alternative Health Services (today called Lyon-Martin Health Services), focusing on lesbian health, opened in 1980 and is still operating today. It was named after Phyllis Lyon and Del Martin, well-known San Francisco lesbian activists who had founded the Daughters of Bilitis in 1955 and helped to form the Council on Religion and the Homosexual in 1964. They were the first same-sex couple to be married when Mayor Gavin Newsom ordered the San Francisco city clerk to issue marriage licenses to such couples in 2004, but that marriage was voided by the state supreme court later that year; when a 2008 state supreme court decision legalized same-sex marriage across California, they were again the first same-sex couple to be married in San Francisco.

figured I'd seen enough penises in the men's HIV prevention materials, why not a beautiful vulva for us? We gave them out after each interview.

The Sluts went to the popular bars and dance clubs, but it was so loud it was difficult to do very many one-on-one interviews before you started to lose your voice. At the time there was a lesbian sex club just getting off the ground—Club Ecstasy. I contacted the producers, Kitaka and Judith, and asked if the Sluts could come do interviews. They were fine with it. The interviews were much easier to do there. We worked the bars and dance clubs weekly and the sex club once a month. We began writing skits, tips and techniques showing how to have safer sex, how to eroticize latex, like attaching a dam to a garter belt, how to double-glove if you went from anal play to the vagina, differences in lube, toys, etc. I'd introduce us, explain the research, and always thank Elizabeth Taylor, founder of amfAR. I'd give a short educational talk, encourage women to be interviewed, and announce the skit.

Along with the interviews we started role-modeling tips or techniques in the bars and dance clubs, too. They'd wear bicycle tights, body suits, or lingerie to stay within the law. The Sluts developed a cult following and definitely created a buzz about women and HIV/STI prevention in the women's community.

Many women came up to us afterwards, thanking us for role-modeling. Many of them were visual learners, so watching "how to" made a huge difference. They'd had a difficult time understanding the "how to" pamphlets. Many appreciated the playful sex- and body-positive delivery of information. I'm getting goosebumps because it was such a powerful time.

When the grant ended the Sluts were still in demand. So I invited all genders, orientations, identities, and proclivities, ages eighteen and up. At one point our age range was eighteen to seventy-six. When people called for a workshop or a performance, we'd be able to represent the audience. Two of my favorite talks still make me smile. We were with Sunday-go-to-church African American moms and their teenage daughters. I called my friend Mary Midget, an African American elder and sassy lesbian comedian, to join the women of color on the team to present the basics of safer sex and some tips and techniques. The other was a special presentation at a national conference of the American Library Association being held in San Francisco. I was contacted and asked to talk at a special education session about the Safer Sex Sluts' unique educational efforts with women. Elizabeth from the Slut team came dressed conservatively and was planted in the audience. I presented some basic amfAR grant and HIV/STI prevention information, and Slut history, and paused as "Marian the Librarian" from *The Music Man* came up over the sound system. Elizabeth stood up and slowly made her way up to the stage, doing a striptease to the music. She was down to a gorgeous negligée top, bikini underwear, and a garter belt that held a dental dam as the song ended, and I said, "This is how we do it!" They went wild! I introduced Elizabeth, we fielded questions, and the women that arranged everything took us out to lunch. It was the best.

The Sluts were writing and performing sketches like "Goldilocks and the Three Barriers" and "Sex Files: The Truth Is Down There." I would love to do something like that with and for elders.

SEX IN HER SEVENTIES

Even though I wasn't looking, I met an older man. We hit it off. He'd lived in a religious order for some years and now lives with a chosen family. The boys he helped raise are grown and married. He had previously never really had a long-term relationship. All those years I'd been talking about sex and sexuality paved the way for me to be an empowered sex- and body-positive old woman. I feel fortunate and am able to challenge the wrongheaded notion that elders are not interested in sex or that we're not sexual.

ADVICE FOR THE NEXT GENERATION

My first thought is *Take care of yourself*. It's interesting that that's the first thing that came to me. Taking care of ourselves is as important as the work we're doing. It is part of the work. Regardless of how old you are, model self-care. You are precious. If you are in a privileged position—and we all are, in one way or another—listen without interrupting, listen deeply, acknowledge your privilege, remain open, and work on that. And yes, sometimes it's really hard, but be flexible, keep your heart open, and maintain a sense of humor. Remember we are the descendants and the ancestors. We can influence the flow of evolution, by risking being part of the change.

STONEWALL AND BISEXUAL ACTIVISM

The most immediate bisexual connection with the Stonewall Rebellion and the post-Stonewall movement was Brenda Howard, a militant New York bisexual activist, a leader of the Gay Liberation Front and Gay Activists Alliance in the early post-Stonewall movement. She was a major figure in planning the one-month Stonewall anniversary rally and coordinating the one-year Christopher Street Liberation Day March to commemorate the first anniversary of the Stonewall Rebellion. This rally and march became the New York City Pride March, which in turn sparked annual Pride celebrations around the world. Brenda originated the idea for a week-long series of events around Pride Day, called Pride Week. She is known as the Mother of Pride. Brenda was an out and outspoken bisexual, a leather activist, sex-positive feminist, polyamorist, and BDSM practitioner. She died of cancer in Queens, New York.

IDENTIFYING WITH THE HUMAN RACE

It [her racial and ethnic identity] has changed over the years. I am Hawai'ian-Japanese-Irish-Polish-Jew, and I was raised Catholic. That used to be my usual: ba-da-bum! And then "mixed-race" felt right, but that quickly became "mixed-blood," and then I was this and then I was that.

I'm at the point where I'm a mixed-heritage human being. It's not that my Hawai'ian or Japanese or Irish or Polish Jew is not important to me. My cultural ties and history are what make me me. I'm especially quickened by my Hawai'ian cultural heritage. I am Kanaka Maoli and actively support the Hawai'ian sovereignty movement. When it comes to race, I'm identifying more with the human race.

Finding Strength

Imani Woody-Macko,
born in Washington, D.C., in 1952

Courtesy of Louis Shackleton

Photographer Louis Shackleton and I met outside Dr. Imani Woody-Macko's office for our first photo shoot together for the book. When she met us at the door with a huge welcoming smile, I knew we were in for something great. Being in her office was like diving into the headquarters of a political campaign. Her space, in the basement of a Metropolitan Community Church, was small and cramped, with piles of leaflets, bumper stickers, proclamations, and folders everywhere. On the bulletin board, the headline from a recent newspaper article, "A Gay Old Time," and three renderings of her dream house spoke to the heart of her work. Imani runs the Diverse Elders Coalition, and on her conference table are the initial drawings of her dream, Mary's House for Older Adults, a residence for fifteen LGBTQ-SGL (same gender loving) older adults, the first of its kind in Washington, DC. It will be located on the property she grew up on in Anacostia, now a predominantly Black community. Imani defines herself as a Black lesbian and a same gender loving person. She is married to Andrea Macko, a native of Jamaica and a communications specialist by skill and education who is currently an electronic programmer for the Department of Defense. I asked her about the 1960s, the early days of the movement, and where she was the night of June 28, 1969. She smiled, and reflected with soft, warm eyes.

STONEWALL BARELY TOUCHED HER LIFE—AT THE TIME

June 28, 1969, . . . I don't . . . it's kind of foggy. I was seventeen. I don't know where I was. I was a senior in high school, definitely not even thinking about Stonewall. Not even a lesbian in my consciousness. Stonewall was not yet relevant for me in my life. It really wasn't relevant then. It's relevant to me now because of the historical context. It didn't touch me then.

FINDING COMMUNITY

My introduction to "the life" happened through African American women's tea parties. Yeah, I found my way in through Lammas, the women's bookstore, Mary Farmer's store. And there was a book review of *Rubyfruit Jungle* in the *Washington Post*. That was a, Wow . . . I had no idea. What? And I'm reading and reading. I see you can buy this book at Lammas! *Wow*. So, that day, I catch the subway—the subway was new at that time—and I catch the subway down to DuPont Circle. And I was working downtown, but I was like, I'ma take a longer lunch!" so I could go to this bookstore. Very scared to go to this bookstore, because they're selling this gay book! Oh, my god! Who's in this bookstore? I went to Lammas and there was this African American woman who said, "Hey, how are you doing?" And I said, "I'm fine. How are you doing?" And that was my entree into what life could be, because I'm wondering, Where are the lesbians? Where are they? How do they find them? Because in my heterosexual married life with a son, how do I find the lesbians?

The tea parties happened mostly on Saturday nights. No alcohol, usually. And that's why they were called tea parties, just tea and conversation and chips, in someone's home. Most of the time in a person's home. The place I remember most was on Florida Avenue. Had nice lights, three stories, different things going on, and all these women. It was awe-inspiring. I mean, I've always liked women.

Lammas was Washington, D.C.'s first women's bookstore and also served as a community center. As a women's space, it had a strong feminist and lesbian focus. Mary Farmer, who became a manager there in 1974 and bought the store in 1976, used it to host concerts and readings by LGBTQ writers. Other independent LGBT bookstores of the time included the Oscar Wilde Bookshop near the Stonewall Inn in New York, Giovanni's Room in Philadelphia, A Different Light in Los Angeles, Charis Books & More in Atlanta, and Lambda Rising in Washington, D.C.

Rita Mae Brown's *Rubyfruit Jungle* was published in 1973 and had sold 250,000 copies by 1977. In it Brown, already known for her political work, told a fictionalized but explicit story of coming out as a lesbian. She worked briefly for the National Organization for Women (NOW), resigning in 1970 over the organization's hostility to lesbians, and was an early member of Redstockings and the Washington lesbian collective The Furies.

Being in the company of women of African descent was a
Wow. They wore slacks, butch-femme mostly. They were
talking about revolution, or womanist theory. And I
developed some friendships from that.

[*I asked Imani if she got together with any girlfriends
there.*] Not from there. I was too scared! Damn, if I could
go back. I was pretty old, all things relative! [*laughs*] I was
in my thirties. But it was a good time to come out! [*laughs*]

[*I asked whether the Black Power movement and the civil
rights movement affected her coming out as a lesbian.*] Yes,
it did. Much more than Stonewall. I started hanging out
with lesbian and same gender identified women who
were, we used to say, "about" something. That just meant
that they had some kind of political consciousness. There
would be a bunch of us that would meet. We would have
picnics at Fort McNair on Friday afternoons after work.
We would meet by Hayne's Point. I became part of a
group, Nubian Women, and there was a social group for
women over thirty-five. We didn't want the babies. Can
you imagine? [*laughs*] Yes. The ageism is insidious! Yes,
it's still there and it's always going to be. I can't imagine it
disappearing. I work hard at doing that.

COMING OUT

I think I've been trying to come out since I was, like,
seven. I wrote this poem for my neighbor. She had these
big breasts and I wrote about her breasts! That's all I

remember. And you know, I'm not that articulate at seven. I'm sure I was somewhat, but. . . . My dad found the poem. My dad asked me, "What is this?" And I said, "We had to write a poem!" He said, "But—" "We had to write a poem!" I told him.

His reaction to that let me know that you should not be writing about women's breasts. That was the first time I tried to come out. I think I've always liked the lesbians, liked the women. Like the women. For me, good conversation is like sex. You first have to have it together [*laughs*] in your head. You know that your brain is the first organ you've got to get through. I've met some wonderful women that I fantasized about, but they had husbands. I had a husband, too. I didn't know you could have a husband and also be a lesbian. That was a disconnect. Oh, the youth of me. And so I've always kind of been there.

My second husband was very smart, and if he had been a woman we would have still been together. He told me, "You know, I think you like women! I really think you do!" I said, "You do?" He said, "Yeah, I think you do!"

That was awesome. He noticed that and he said that out loud, but he didn't really mean for me to know that or act on that. After he opened it up to me, I opened it up to me, and yeah, it was true. And so we parted ways after some time. We had a good divorce. We went to the hearing together, went out to dinner, visited some friends, let folks know. Amazing. And we still talk. But he was the first one that said, "You know, I think you like women."

SEX IN HER YOUNGER YEARS

We all remember the first woman. The first woman. I was wearing a pendant and she just touched the pendant. And the electrical shocks, I said, What the—? Oh, my god! [*snaps fingers*] And, wow! Even thinking about it now, that was great sex. Great and plentiful. It seemed like I had more energy when I was in my thirties and forties than I have now. But I don't know. More, more. There were times where we'd eat and sleep and—can I say?— eat, fuck, sleep, eat, fuck . . . that was the weekend! "Did you have a good weekend?" "Yeah! [*laughs*] It was good. Had a great weekend." [*laughs*] And now, I wouldn't consider that a great weekend. That would be a good weekend, but I have to get some other stuff in. I think we might go back to that weekend thing. Maybe. I do have an eighty-three-year-old living with us, my step-mom, so maybe not. But, oh, maybe.

MARRYING HER LOVE

Oh, my goodness. Andrea is the sweetest person. And she's a bear. She is. When people talk with her or interact with her, she doesn't take a whole lot of bullshit. She doesn't mean to be sharp, but she can be. She loves me, unconditionally, with conditions. [*laughs*] As I do her. [*laughs*] We got married here [*at the Metropolitan Community Church*]. The first time, we had a holy union in 2005.

And then, when marriage became legal in Washington, we had a small ceremony upstairs in the chapel. Pastor Dwayne from the MCC officiated for the legal ceremony. But we call 2005 our real marriage. So we had two ministers. Andrea's minister Sophia Sumpter and Phil Matthews from this church.

LOVING HER WIFE, ANDREA

We do some sexing, but have been around and with each other so long and so deep that when we're together intimately, it's pretty much planned with cool sheets, good nectar, sexy music, and perfumed bodies. My baby is hot with or without clothes! Sometimes we tap those early sexual memories and do do-overs. Yaass. Breathless. Can't wait till she's back home. I've got the lilac sheets on the bed, candles waiting to be lit, and some little "fun snack."

LESSONS FROM HER PARENTS

I think my dad's work ethic would be part of my character. He was a very strict guy, and he had a work ethic: You do what you say you're going to do. Your word is your bond. You do your best. No one can ask for more than that. You do your best at whatever it is. You're going to sweep the floor, do it the best. Whatever it is, if you're going to half-ass it, don't do it! Somebody else can come along and do a better job.

So that was part of it. My mom died when I was ten, but she imparted in me the love of learning and being. I thought I could do anything. I was her first kid and I became the helper. I had four siblings. I got a library card at four. My mom fought the system for me to get into school earlier. That's why I was graduating earlier and that's why I could already read. I could already do all this other stuff. That was very telling for me. A Black woman in the system, fighting the system to get her kid into school. That was a great lesson I took with me in raising my child: if there was something that I thought that he should have, that I could fight and get it done. It never occurred to me that I could fight and lose. Her willingness to take them on—a lion. You know, talk about a tiger mom!

THE IMPORTANCE OF EDUCATION

That was a hard road. I got my master's late in life. And I said, I need to keep going. I need to keep going because if I don't keep going, I won't do it. And so there were three of us who made a pact to get our PhD, and I'm the only one that kept the promise. I was so mad with myself that these other two women dropped it. They just could! They could drop out, and they don't have that big school loan, and they don't have the seven years of heartache. They just were able to say, "I made another choice and I'm giving this up." I feel like I don't—with my baggage, my background—I really did not have that luxury, to give up.

My dissertation was on African American gay and lesbian elders and their access to health care. That's what led me to Mary's House.

For my mother, education was the best. And being a Black person in the United States, that's one way that you could excel. With education. That's how I could see her shining. I have an uncle, my uncle Jasper, and he said, your pop would be so proud of you, so don't stop. I did it all through, even with deaths. My sister died while I was doing that and I had papers to do, and you know, you just do it.

TEACHING GERIATRIC NURSES ABOUT OLDER ADULTS AND SEX

I did a training for some nurses that talked about sexuality for residents. And talked about folks still wanting to have sex. It's a need. Sometimes you can see people trying to take care of their own needs with spoons and stuff that really hurts them, so I tell them, "Let's get on board and get them some real toys." And they wanted to throw me out because they didn't know I was going to go that deep! They just thought I was going to say . . . You know, we had some case studies about, you know, if a resident puts a sign on their door that says "Do Not Disturb," and they're in there with another person, what do you do? You stay out! This is their home. This is their room!

RACISM, SEXISM, HOMOPHOBIA

We've gone far. When I do workshops, there's a picture I show, a cartoon, and it has stages of movements, and it shows acceptance at the top and denial at the bottom. It has civil rights almost at the top, women's rights at the top, LGBT marriage equality rights at the bottom. So, as with all movements, we'll move up. That is my hope. That is my kind of knowledge. My gut feeling. That discrimination can't last. It just cannot. I think we will prevail. We are working on it. Resist. Resist! I have a friend, Joy Silver, who's running for State Senate out in California. And, awesome. Awesome. And in a little county in Palm Springs. How they became a sanctuary city, and all this kind of stuff. My friends are doing stuff like that all over the country. I've been an activist all my adult life, yes. I used to take my baby on my back to meetings and give him little crayons. I had an independent school when he was a baby, in my house. Yes, so I've been an activist.

RISKS SHE HAS FACED

Risks: being a woman. Risks: being a Black woman. Risks: being a lesbian. Being a mother. Being a wife. Being a femme. Being an activist. Being an older woman. Being a sexual being.

I'll share a risk. In this revolutionary time, I was hanging out with all these Black women. And I was advocating open relationships [*laughs*], but that was not part and parcel of being a revolutionary. "What is that? What does that mean?" And I said, "What it means is that I don't cheat. It means that I love at least two women." I don't know whether I love them equally, but I love them a lot. I'm open and honest. And we would get together and have these feeling checks, and so we really were a family. It was polyamory, but not, because I didn't know that word then. No, they were not calling it that yet. So that was a risk. And to still be the stand-up Black woman, Black lesbian that I am. So I took some guff from that. [*laughs*]

Being a femme is a risk. That tide is turning because there are some young femmes that identify. But being a femme, what does that mean? You're not strong. Being a butch, what does that mean? Because when you're naked it doesn't have anything to do with what your clothing is. But to instill that, to impart that information to others now. Because I don't even say it. I just am. You just look at me and if you don't have a problem, I don't have a problem. It's more telling when I'm with my partner. I mean I'm invisible in the real world. Especially because I'm a grandmother too. Grandmother. "Lesbians don't have grandkids. They don't have sex." I'm really invisible. I was somewhere, and I said, "My wife." And the person, you could see they were puzzled. And this was recent; this was yesterday. I was interviewing a person to help care for my mother and I said my wife was in Greenland. And you could tell her little self was trying to wrap her head around it. She said, "I beg your pardon?" and I said, "My wife." She said, "Ohh, OK . . ." You know, she tried to get with it. But that happens often. I say it often, just for that.

MARY'S HOUSE

My dad. He became ill and he had a stroke. He never fully recovered from that stroke. We put him in a continuing care retirement community. It was a good one. He's a middle-class guy and he had put a couple of pennies together, so we didn't have to go the Medicaid route. We went to one that was respected. But they didn't know who he was. They didn't know that he was Reverend Woody. He was a minister at Mt. Carmel Baptist Church. In his later years, he was more like a traveling evangelist, going from one storefront church to another. They didn't know him. They might have known, but it didn't register for them. For them, he was Room 232 and he had needs to be met. We just pulled him out, you know, because dying at home is a good thing. He died in 2010.

So that was one of the things that made me think. When he died, he left me my childhood home. What to do with this? And part of it was [wanting] a place where my father could have been acknowledged as an older person, as opposed to a number. Creating some kind of communal living around it. I wonder what would have happened had he been a gay man? An out, openly gay man? Or a transgender person? Or an out lesbian? I wonder what kind of service he may have gotten. You know, room number 232 might have changed, but I think there might have been some homophobia.

The house is on Anacostia Road, the house I grew up in. When I lived here, there were six or seven houses up here. We were the first Black family. Then white flight happened. Then the apartment buildings happened, but my dad kept his house. When he died, he left me the house. So we're going to tear it down and build Mary's House. We'll have a garden, which we'll call the Stonewall Garden to give a nod to Stonewall. It'll have a walking path up here as well. There will be the yellow brick

SAGE CEO Michael Adams awards Imani an Advocacy Award for Excellence on Aging. Courtesy of Cathy Renna

road, because folks were "friends of Dorothy," which meant you were gay back in the 1930s and 1940s. People in the Mattachine Society used that phrase a lot, "friends of Dorothy." To help us raise funds, you can buy a brick in honor of someone, on the yellow brick road.

Mary's House is more than just building that house. We have two programs. One program does a home match, because people want to stay in their homes. One of the people has to be sixty-five. Both of the people have to be either gay or gay-friendly, one of those. That's how we do a home match. The other program is the house itself, a model for housing celebrating the whole person as they age, no matter who they are. We are creating independent, communal housing for older adults to eliminate the intense isolation experienced due to aging and sexual or gender identity or orientation. And we would love to have people contribute to our work.

What gives me strength? Cheerios. [*laughs*] Spinach. I know, right? That is too funny. And I'm laughing because it's really hard to think what gives me strength, you know? Where do the strong go, when it's tough? Well, you know they say seven years and you want to leave your spouse? I'm wondering if this is my seventh year and I want to leave this project! I can't. We're at the place where we've jumped through all the governmental hoops, we've jumped through the zoning hoops, we've jumped through all the things that we need to jump through to build this two-million-dollar house. When we started off, we thought we were going have eight rooms, and now we're going to have fifteen rooms. The eight rooms was going to be $1.5 million; the fifteen rooms is $2.3 million. They're all the same. [*laughs*] I don't have it in my hip pocket so it's all the same! But I understand that in the scope of building, it's not any money. So once I understand that it's not any money, we just need to raise that money. And hey, that's what we'll do. We'll raise that money.

TWELVE PAIRS OF BLACK SHOES

My advice to young people? I wish I'd saved more money. [*laughs*] Let me just say that off the top. I would have saved more money by now, because you will get to be sixty-five. I thought I was going to be dead at thirty-five and I'm still living, so I didn't plan for that. So that would be something for young folks to know. Because most of us don't have enough money to live if we would live to be a hundred. And in the seventh inning of my life, I want to be comfortable. You know, living like I'm living now, doing this activist work, not doing a nine-to-five job, I don't need as much money. But I wish I had figured that out earlier. That I don't need twelve pair of black shoes. That I love. Oh, gosh. But I don't need twelve pair of black shoes, right? I don't need to be the collector of . . . whatever. That costs money, to collect these things.

To be honest, like down deep within my core, just show my authentic self, no matter what the price. That's what I struggle with now. I mean, what you see is what you get. But I would love to go deeper and not dye my hair. And not do these things that I feel ageism is pressing me to do.

CONFRONTING AGEISM

You know, when you fill out forms, it just goes to sixty-five. [*laughs*] Just so you know! You don't notice till you get down there, you know . . . when it's "18–25," "25–40," "40–65," the end. [*laughs*] At times, I mean, I have to work so hard to be visible. I mean, I work fucking hard. I have to be at all meetings. When I was younger, I could be at some meetings, because my stuff was out, and it carried. Now I have to stand up taller, speak louder, refer to myself as Dr. Woody all the time, so that I don't have to work that hard. You know, color my hair. It's a lot of work, aging. To be heard and not be invisible. I'm feeling poorly this week, and there was a meeting I wanted to attend with the Office on Aging. And I just got sick; I couldn't go. I'm a co-chair of another meeting, and I should have

> The Diverse Elders Coalition comprises five national organizations that work to improve the experience of aging for racially, ethnically, and sexually diverse people by promoting policies and programs that remove barriers and help older adults live full and active lives.

gone in, and I didn't go. I know that I can't be sick the next time. You know, I don't have that luxury, I can't do that. I have to be out there doing that, even though I had a board member go in my place. It wasn't like Mary's House was not represented. And he did a good job. But I wasn't there.

I have to write. Well, you know, in academia you have to write. I mean, because you're a nobody. I didn't go to school to write! [*laughs*] I love to write. I love it. But I don't know what to say. At one point I was really prolific. But now . . . I'm tired! I'm tired! Damn, I don't feel like writing anything. I write for the Diverse Elders, I write for this one, I write for that one . . . but it's "Dr. Woody!" That . . . [*groans*] Leave me alone. [*laughs*]

TAKING A KNEE

We really didn't get a chance to talk about racism much. You did mention that many folks, African Americans, thought about the civil rights movement more than the gay rights movement. And that is playing itself out in the Colin Kaepernick thing. For me, it's a full monty. It's that the young man kneeled because of racism and police brutality. I'm so clear on that. It's not wrapped up in the anthem and the flag. I have colleagues, friends, and acquaintances who are Caucasian, who write things like, "Let's stop doing this, it doesn't matter whether they stand or kneel, let's just talk about the devastation from the hurricane

In the fall of 2016 Colin Kaepernick, a quarterback for the San Francisco 49ers, began to kneel while the national anthem was played before games, to protest racial injustice and police violence against Black men and other people of color. (For the first two weeks he sat, but he switched to kneeling in order to show respect for members of the military while still protesting.) His protest inspired dozens of other athletes to similarly protest, by taking a knee or otherwise, during the anthem, but also triggered fierce reactions and a great deal of debate. Kaepernick knelt during the anthem before every game that season. He opted out of his contract with the 49ers at the end of the year, becoming a free agent, but has not been signed by another team since. Both he and his 49ers teammate Eric Reid, the first to join him in protesting, filed collusion grievances with the NFL; both cases were settled under confidential terms.

In February 1965, civil rights leaders Rev. Dr. Martin Luther King Jr. and Dr. Ralph Abernathy, along with nearly eight hundred nonviolent freedom fighters, took a knee and were arrested in a protest against voting rights restrictions, racist violence, and poverty in Selma, Alabama.

in Puerto Rico." I haven't responded, but I know that I have to respond to these people, the ones that I consider friends—the other ones I don't have to—but the ones I consider friends, I have to respond to that. And it's just, all the Black folks that I know, they get it. It's about America, the United States not fulfilling its promise. And that's all. One knee down? King used to do a knee. King used to do a knee, Abernathy, you know, all of those boys, when they were doing that, going down on a knee was the thing.

Colin did that accidentally, actually. Before this knee thing started, a white guy who was active military wrote to Colin and said something like, "I want to understand this. I want to listen with an open mind because I can't ever say I know what being Black is." That I understand. Like somebody saying they know what war is and they've never been in combat. So it was a great letter he wrote to Colin, and Colin had him come up and they had a ninety-minute conversation. And talked. Colin explained that he sat it out when they played the national anthem. He sat in a chair. But nobody noticed. But the guy said, "You know, kneeling would be a better thing. On one knee, because when a person is buried in the military, they wrap the flag thirteen times and then the person that presents the flag, presents it on a knee." So he said, "I would feel better if you knelt." Colin said, "That's what I'll do." So that's the story. Some folks that I know researched kneeling, what it is saying, what it's not saying. It's peaceful protest.

THE FIGHT IS VISIBLE AND INVISIBLE

I get tired of peaceful protest because nothing really happens. Stonewall wasn't peaceful. And it was the linchpin that changed our world. The Tea Party wasn't peaceful. The linchpin that changed this from being a colony. People don't give up power. Racism is right up there. Racism, sexism, and then homophobia. So for me, it's way down. It's third on the list, and sometimes it's not on the list at all. People get it; it's Washington, DC. Folks get that. Homophobia's not much of a problem today. But racism? Sexism? That is so alive and well, and that's the fight, invisible and visible, that I fight every day.

CHAPTER EIGHT

Postscript: Working with Elders in the Community

Joey Wasserman, born in Hong Kong in 1985

Courtesy of Louis Shackleton

Joey Wasserman lives in New York City. In his thirties, he's certainly not an elder, but I've included him as a postscript because he works for SAGE: Advocacy and Services for LGBT Elders. He wouldn't be doing the great work that he does if not for the struggles of the LGBTQ activists who came before him.

Joey has had an unusual upbringing. He was born in Hong Kong and adopted by Harriette and Ted Wasserman, a Jewish couple in Philadelphia, Pennsylvania. In May of 1977, his parents bought a gay bar called the Venture Inn, right in the middle of the "gayborhood," the LGBTQ part of Philadelphia. Joey grew up familiar with the staff and patrons and comfortable in the gay community, and he came out himself in high school. After graduating in 2008 from York College in York, Pennsylvania, he worked in an LGBT center for York Planned Parenthood, for the Jewish Community Center in York, and for the Human Rights Campaign in Washington, DC, before joining the staff of SAGE in New York City. Joey is handsome, he's deep and expressive, and he speaks with passion about his work and his convictions. He describes himself as gay, Chinese, and Jewish. As soon as I met him, I sensed he had an important story to tell about the power of Stonewall and what it means in his life as a gay man.

WORKING AT SAGE

Why am I working at SAGE? That's a good question. I ask myself that all the time. I think it's rooted in my upbringing. I grew up with a very affirming family, with parents who were closely tied into the LGBTQ community in Philadelphia. My parents knew about me being gay before I did. They were never shy about exposing or engaging me in the gay culture. I was sixteen when we had conversations about my sexual orientation. But it was super casual and based on a guy I was dating at the time.

Growing up, I learned a lot about the LGBTQ community, especially the history, and that really piqued my

Ted Wasserman (center) surrounded by
employees of the Venture Inn: Bob
Caulkens, aka Mabel Redtop (left), David
Christopher (on floor), and Lenny Cooney
(right). Courtesy of Joey Wasserman

interest. I continued my interest into advocacy work—
from starting Lambda, the LGBT student group at York
College, to interning for Hillary Clinton during the 2008
Democratic presidential primaries, to working at HRC
[*the Human Rights Campaign*], upwards to SAGE.

AGE IS A TABOO TOPIC

In terms of activism, there's a lot of growth that needs
to happen in the LGBTQ community on many different

levels, specifically related to diversity and equity. We must recognize that diversity stretches beyond race and gender and includes faith, socioeconomic background, age, and social identities. Age in particular is a huge factor that not a lot of people address these days, whether you're gay or straight or on the continuum there. It's considered a topic that's taboo, because people don't want to see themselves as aging. Our culture often values youth over wisdom and experience.

Conversely, ageism affects younger people, too. Young people or those perceived as being young tend to be treated in an unfavorable way precisely because of their youth. At some point, we become victims of ageism on both sides of the spectrum.

IMPACT OF THE STONEWALL REBELLION

I think the sacrifices that they've [*those who fought at Stonewall*] made shouldn't be in vain. It is essential to continue raising awareness and visibility about critical moments in our history, so we may learn from it. They were visible during a time when it was much harder, I believe, than what I'm going through, or what future generations might go through. I come across many LGBTQ adults who share their stories. Their stories are very fascinating because I think a lot of people view LGBTQ history through the lens of oppression, but there's a lot of vibrancy in that community as well. That story needs to be told because that's the driving force in our movement! The courage, the energy, and the sacrifices that so many of our elders made were for a reason. And a reason that we should never forget.

DISCRIMINATION AGAINST LGBTQ ELDERS

The process of coming out never ends, and no two people follow the same coming out paths. Some are lucky to have the support of their family and friends, others are forced out of the closet, and for many people it only happens after decades of struggling to reconcile their sexuality and/or gender before ultimately coming out later in life. There are many LGBTQ elders I've met over the years that have come out in their forties, fifties, and sixties; it's often complex, involving previous marriages and families. And all too often, opening the door for the first time, stepping into the LGBTQ community by navigating the bar scene or the Internet leaves much to be desired.

For many individuals in our community, sometimes it doesn't get better, especially when entering long-term care facilities. Eldercare facilities are often unwelcoming towards LGBTQ older adults, forcing many back into the closet, and that's sad. Take, for instance, nursing homes; these are challenging environments for our elders. Many are sharing residences with individuals who harbor bias against them, or it may be the facility's staff who are not equipped to care for this population of elders.

SEX IN HIS THIRTIES

Do I have sexual needs? Of course! Like anyone else. As I get older, I put more emphasis on building a relationship than a one-night stand, but I do love my fun. I want to come to a moment and realize, this is the person I want to spend the rest of my life with. This is the person I want to build memories with.

I consider myself privileged. Especially with the understanding of our history and recognizing sacrifices made by so many who have fought for us to love who we want, no matter what. In recent years, since the legalization of same-sex marriage, I've noticed more of my friends in long-term committed relationships and a few getting married. These relationships are important because future generations are directly dependent on the role models of today. As for me, right now my main focus is my job—being a strong independent man.

HAVING AN IMPACT ON OTHERS

Whether you like it or not, we're all getting older. But the aging process is different for everyone, and how you embrace it will determine your life's trajectory. As a younger gay man, I don't think about it all too often. But I do notice it can be a point of internal struggle for many in our community, both young and old. Ultimately, it's not our thoughts, emotions, or words that define us but the impact we have on others, our community, and the world. It starts with knowing your values and understanding that they will evolve over time as a function of an ever-changing environment. That it's OK to challenge preconceived notions and instead explore new ideas to help form your values and ignite your passions.

Aging in general isn't seen as terribly sexy, let alone in the LGBTQ community. But over the years, I have realized that age is just a number and our community offers so much more in depth, richness, and vibrancy. This realization didn't come overnight, but I saw it over time and started to appreciate that we are strongest when we're united.

Putting words into action, I have made it central to my life to impart knowledge and awareness regarding age and intergenerational engagement to those who I surround myself with. This includes involving my friends in campaigns and events I produce on behalf of SAGE. Not only do they see the value in supporting those who have come before us, but they also enjoy hearing their stories and learning more about our collective history. And at its core, after decades of discrimination and harassment, many celebrate the openness and campiness of our elders, our friends. Whether it's going to Julius, a historic LGBTQ bar in the Village or visiting Shawn & Nick's Courtyard Café, an LGBTQ diner in Fort Lauderdale, whenever I'm in town—there's always someone with a story to tell and a lesson to be learned.

These are the types of environments I grew up in. It wasn't unusual to hear the banter, silliness, and friendly insults between two old queens in my parents' restaurant and bar when I was growing up. I used to work there from time to time and I loved it! So many characters and dynamic personalities that can only be found in an LGBTQ bar. Also, there's a unique comfort of open criticism specific to the older LGBTQ population that isn't prevalent amongst the younger generation. It's very similar to what you would find in a Jewish deli in the 1950s and 1960s, the shared history of persecution and finding the laughter through tears.

THE VALUE OF STORIES

Storytelling is one of the most powerful ways to breathe life into a movement and to draw on the unique life experiences of our LGBTQ elders. It gives us an opportunity to showcase the events, places, and people that have been instrumental in defining our community. It is important to remember the emergence of the Mattachine Society, that fateful night in 1969, the LGBTQ revolution of the 1970s, the AIDS epidemic of the 1980s, up to marriage equality and how we can make sure future generations never forget.

I come across a lot of younger people in the LGBTQ community who are unaware of the sacrifices made by our pioneers. Many seem to know and care more about sex, celebrities, and the latest phone apps than wisdom and knowledge from our past. It's sad, but it's true. In the words of George Santayana, "Those who cannot remember the past are condemned to repeat it."

CHAPTER NINE

Continuing Their Legacies

In the course of my doctoral research, I researched sexual satisfaction in older adults ages sixty to seventy-five who were in same-gender relationships and, through a series of questions in an online format, analyzed the results. Once I completed my statistical analyses, I immediately noticed that the results did not fit the stereotypes we have for older adults. I found that, contrary to what the media might have us believe, many LGBTQ elders are having sex and are feeling pretty good about it. Of course not all LGBTQ elders are in same-gender relationships; many are single, having sex or in relationships with someone of another gender (including bi and trans people). The 265 participants in my survey research were from a non-random sample of women and men who were recruited online and were from the United States and Canada. (I used the word relationship rather than couple to allow for any form of monogamous or non-monogamous configurations. Instead of asking only people who had been in a relationship longer than a specified period of time, I intentionally wanted to leave that open, to include those who were in the early stages as well as those in longer-term relationships. What I hadn't expected was that I was unable to capture data from people who had recently become single after losing their long-term partner. I was only able to conduct analyses of two genders (women and men); I was unable to collect enough data from other genders to be statistically significant.

Another aspect of the Stonewall Generation that was particularly fascinating was their religious background and the evolution of their religious affiliation or lack thereof. More than half of the participants reported that the religion they were brought up in was either Protestant (35 percent) or Catholic (23 percent). When asked what (if any) religion they currently identify with, the percentages for Protestants/Christians and Catholics dropped dramatically. Almost half were not religious (48 percent) and, of those who currently identified with a religion, Unitarian Universalism increased. And it is no wonder. The Catholic Church and many Christian denominations caused many of these members of the Stonewall Generation to struggle with their religious and sexual identities as they were coming out.

My doctoral research is part of a growing body of literature around older adults' sexuality. However, there is still scant research about older LGBTQ adults' sexuality. That is a direction I would like to see pursued by future sexuality researchers.

At first, I thought I'd be interviewing people who'd all been at Stonewall, but that proved more difficult than I imagined. Many of those Stonewall veterans are now gone. Marsha P. Johnson died in 1992 and Stormé DeLarverie died in 2014.

Each of the people identified in the book was willing to take risks by talking to a sexuality researcher about their lives. As I reflect on these conversations, I discover a few themes.

1. **Others knowing first.** It often took someone close to them, usually their ex-wives or ex-husbands or parents, to notice they were gay, lesbian, or bisexual, and it was amazing how those closest to them understood who they were often before they knew themselves. David's wife, Imani's husband, Lani's boyfriend, and Joey's parents all knew first.

2. **The importance of place.** Where they lived and finding a community have been very important to many LGBTQ people with certain cities creating more of a draw. Mandy, Miss Major, and Joey all moved to New York City. Mandy and Miss Major also moved to San Francisco. Mandy said she had to leave a rural area to be in New York City and then San Francisco to find other lesbians.

3. **The centrality of bars.** Back in the 1960s and 1970s, bars were the primary place to meet people if you were gay, lesbian, bisexual, or transgender. David explains what Stonewall meant to him as a young gay man. Miss Major describes the bars that felt comfortable to her and her girls. Mandy talks about the significance of a lesbian-owned set of bars in San Francisco, Maud's and Amelia's. The owner was influential to the rest of the community, and the bars themselves were a kind of home for many lesbians. Hardy talks about finding the leather bars in Dallas as key to his coming out process. Aside from bookstores and coffeehouses, bars like Stonewall were central to the community.

4. **The powerful role of religion.** Although religion has played such a negative role in so many LGBTQ peoples' lives, later choosing a religion has played a positive role in many of their lives. Imani is part of the MCC church in Washington, D.C., and the MCC minister officiated at her wedding to her wife. Hardy is part of a leather pew in a large LGBTQ church in Dallas, Texas. Mandy has been involved with the Quakers through the War Resisters League.

5. **Commitment to activism.** Stonewall wasn't the only thing that helped direct them to a life of passionate activism. Not all were solely politicized by Stonewall or the LGBTQ rights movement. Other movements seemed just as pivotal, including the anti-war

movement of the 1960s, and the women's, the Civil Rights, and human rights movements. Each of the elders I interviewed has been involved in at least one social change political movement. Most have marched, rallied, and organized not only for LGBTQ political rights but for other issues as well. When Joey expresses the importance of remembering past political struggles so we never forget, it's worth reflecting on the wide array of major social movements that the people I interviewed have been involved in: David Velasco Bermudez's quest to teach young people about Stonewall; Mandy Carter's decades of work for the War Resisters League, her leadership in Black progressive organizations like Southerners On New Ground and the National Black Justice Coalition, and her work with young people in Asheville, North Carolina; Edie Daly's work educating intergenerational groups of older lesbians and young queer cisgender women; Miss Major Griffin-Gracy's fight to reduce the incarceration of transgender people in the U.S. prison system; Hardy Haberman's crusade against sexual violence in the leather community; Bob Isadore's leadership of the Democratic Party in his part of Massachusetts; Lani Ka'ahumanu's early involvement supporting the United Farmworkers, and Black Panther Party, Anti-Vietnam War organizing, and her work on sex education and leadership to reduce biphobia; Jackie

Mirkin's work on poverty in Newark, New Jersey; and Imani Woody-Macko's passion to create housing for LGBT-SGL elders in Washington D.C.

6. **Divisions within the LGBTQ community.** Based on the rigid, binary notions of sexual orientation of the 1970s and 1980s, another theme I uncovered was the sting of divisiveness. As liberating as coming out was for some of the individuals in this book, it was often tinged with painful and long-lasting divisions within the community: the challenges of not being enough or of being too much, not lesbian enough, not gay enough, too butch, too femme. Lani's stories about coming out to throngs of cheering lesbians the first time and then social ostracism from those same women when she came out later as bi are all too common. Miss Major articulates the need for more visibility and power for trans people. Joey and Imani speak of the need for more inclusivity and acceptance of aging in the community.

7. **Difficulty talking about sex.** Even with someone who is trained as a sexuality professional, it was hard for people to talk about sex. Not unlike the rest of our population, these individuals found it easier to talk about other issues like aging or coming out than talking about sex.

8. **Resilience.** The people I interviewed have been harassed, ostracized, fired. They've lost their children, their families. Though many of them experienced discrimination at work, at home, and with family

members and have had to repress their authentic sexualities for decades, their resilience seemed quite high.

9. **Focus on orientation over gender.** The current focus on gender identity among younger people is not as prevalent for LGBTQ elders. While Joey was used the question, "What pronouns do you use?" many of the older adults were more accustomed to talking about their sexual orientation than their gender identity. Miss Major made a significant contribution to this discussion by asking why the "T" in the LGBTQ movement is always at the back of the list even though transgender people were in the forefront of the early days of the movement.

10. **Dreaming of a place to call home.** So often, LGBTQ elders have little or no family to fall back on as they age. Imani's dream of creating a matching program and a residence for LGBTQ elders is akin to Miss Major's ideas for a compound where trans women can be together for comfort, safety, political education, and joy.

11. **Old in age, young in spirit.** There are so many laughs in these interviews, and many had an incredible ability to laugh at themselves. Many of the people I interviewed seemed so spirited and fired up about the topics we discussed and the book itself as a vehicle for education and advocacy. Their internalizations of the homophobia they had experienced seemed quite low at this point in their lives.

And eureka, many of these themes mirror the results of my quantitative research on sexual satisfaction, relationship satisfaction, resilience, and internalized homophobia. It is my hope that this book helps to illuminate some truths and create understanding about the lives of LGBTQ elders. In this way, this book can be a useful tool, especially (to use the phrase of the Creating Change conference) in the "tyrannical times" we are living in now, with racism, xenophobia, homophobia, transphobia, sexual violence, and other oppressive forces being turned from tweets to public policy by a president wantonly bent on destroying our constitutional rights.

Whether young or old (or somewhere in between), many of us are looking for something that can remind us of a time of great political change and cultural upheaval. The movements of the 1960s and 1970s have been integral to the development of more than one generation.

I've spent more than three years conducting interviews for this book and writing about LGBTQ elders who came of age at the time of Stonewall. Working with them and a fantastic group of photographers to gather portraits was invigorating and gave me hope. Now that you've been introduced to this group of LGBTQ elders, I hope you share my sense of the excitement and I hope you agree with me that given the dearth of research focused on LGBTQ elders, these stories need to be heard.

Each of the people I interviewed entered adulthood through a different door, and each of these LGBTQ elders came out, struggled, had people who were important to them, had people who hurt them, and had their own individual paths and truths. If you can find hope in their stories to continue their legacies, then I will have succeeded. These are ordinary people who have lived—and are living—through extraordinary times. It is up to all of us to continue their legacies.

Resources

ORGANIZATIONS

Diverse Elders Coalition   diverseelders.org

Highlander Research and Education Center
    highlandercenter.org

Griffin-Gracy Historical Retreat and Education Center
    houseofggs.org

Lesbian Herstory Archives   lesbianherstoryarchives.org

Making Gay History   makinggayhistory.com

Mary's House for Older Adults   maryshousedc.org

National Black Justice Coalition   nbjc.org

National LGBTQ Task Force   thetaskforce.org

National Resource Center on LGBT Aging
    lgbtagingcenter.org

New York City LGBT Historical Sites Project
    nyclgbtsites.org

Old Lesbian Oral Herstory Project   olohp.org

Older Lesbians Organizing for Change   oloc.org

Our Better Half   **ourbetterhalf.net**
Our Whole Lives Sexuality Education for Older Adults
   uua.org/re/owl
SAGE: Advocacy and Services for LGBT Elders
   sageusa.org
Sexuality and Aging Consortium of Widener University
   sexualityandaging.com
Southerners on New Ground   **southernersonnewground.org**
Stonewall Veterans Association   **stonewallvets.org**
Transgender Gender-Variant & Intersex Justice Project
   tgijp.org
Woodhull Sexual Freedom Alliance
   woodhullfoundation.org

BOOKS

Barker, Meg-John and Julia Scheele. *Queer: A Graphic History.*
   London: Icon Books, 2016.
Bornstein, Kate and S. Bear Bergman. *Gender Outlaws: The
   Next Generation.* New York: Seal Press, 2010.
Bronski, Michael. *A Queer History of the United States.* Boston:
   Beacon Press, 2012.
Burleson, William. *Bi America: Myths, Truths, and Struggles of
   an Invisible Community.* Abingdon: Routledge, 2005.
Carter, David. *Stonewall: The Riots That Sparked the Gay
   Revolution.* New York: Griffin, 2010.
Chauncey, George. *Gay New York: Gender, Urban Culture, and
   the Making of the Gay Male World 1890–1940.* New York:
   Basic Books, 2008.

Daly, Edie. *Old Lesbian Memory Quilt: Stories Told by Edie Daly on Her 80th Birthday*. Amherst, MA: Modern Memoirs, Inc., 2019.

Eisner, Shiri. *Bi: Notes for a Bisexual Revolution*. New York: Seal Press, 2013.

Eversmeyer, Arden and Margaret Purcell. *Without Apology: Old Lesbian Life Stories*. Houston: Old Lesbian Oral Herstory Project, 2012.

———. *Odd Girls and Twilight Lovers: A History of Lesbian Life in Twentieth-Century America*. New York: Columbia University Press, 2012.

Feinberg, Leslie. *Trans Liberation: Beyond Pink or Blue*. Boston: Beacon Press, 1999.

Haberman, Hardy. *The Family Jewels: A Guide to Male Genital Play and Torment*. Emeryville, CA: Greenery Press, 2001.

Harrad, Kate, ed. *Claiming the B in LGBT*. Portland, OR: Thorntree Press, 2018.

Henderson, Mae G. & Johnson, E. Patrick, eds. *Black Queer Studies: A Critical Anthology*. Durham, NC: Duke University Press, 2005.

Johnson, E. Patrick, ed. *No Tea, No Shade: New Writings in Black Queer Studies*. Durham, NC: Duke University Press, 2016.

Kaʻahumanu, Lani. *My Grassroots are Showing: Stories, Speeches and Special Affections*. (forthcoming, see lanikaahumanu.com for updates)

Kaʻahumanu, Lani and Loraine Hutchins. *Bi Any Other Name: Bisexual People Speak Out*. New York: Riverdale Avenue Books, 2015.

Mogul, Joey L., Andrea J. Ritchie, and Kay Whitlock. *Queer (In)Justice: The Criminalization of LGBT People in the United States*. Boston: Beacon Press, 2012.

New York Public Library. *The Stonewall Reader*. New York: Penguin Classics, 2019.

Ochs, Robyn. *Getting Bi: Voices of Bisexuals Around the World*. Boston: Bisexual Resource Center, 2009.

Pharr, Suzanne. *Homophobia: A Weapon of Sexism*. Little Rock, AR: Women's Project, 1997.

Rajunov, Micah and A. Scott Duane. *Nonbinary: Memoirs of Gender and Identity*. New York: Columbia University Press, 2019.

Reimer, Matthew and Leighton Brown. *We Are Everywhere: Protest, Power, and Pride in the History of Queer Liberation*. New York: Ten Speed Press, 2019.

Ryan, Hugh, *When Brooklyn Was Queer*. New York: St. Martin's Press, 2019.

Snorton, C. Riley. *Black on Both Sides: A Racial History of Trans Identity*. Minneapolis: University of Minnesota Press, 2017.

Somerville, Siobhan B. *Queering the Color Line*. Durham, NC: Duke University Press, 2000.

Stryker, Susan. *Transgender History: The Roots of Today's Revolution*. New York: Seal Press, 2017.

Wilchins, Riki. *TRANS/gressive: How Transgender Activists Took On Gay Rights, Feminism, the Media, and Congress . . . and Won!* New York: Riverdale Avenue Books, 2017.

Acknowledgments

Thanks to all the people who graciously gave me their time, their stories, and their perspectives. You are truly a gift. David Velasco Bermudez, Mandy Carter, Edie Daly, Miss Major Griffin-Gracy, Hardy Haberman, Robert Isadore, Lani Ka'ahumanu, Jackie Mirkin, Joey Wasserman, and Imani Woody-Macko, thank you for your trust in me with your words. Tremendous thanks to Hugh Ryan for his valuable assistance in historical content and enormous appreciation to Mykal Slack, Adam Dyer, and Kimberley Debus, who greatly improved my thinking through multiple lenses of race, gender, and sexual identities. My heartfelt thanks go to my dear friend and editor, Barbara Deinhardt, whose questions and ideas helped me enormously. To Sally Bellerose for her encouraging words and faith in me, Shana Sureck for saying yes to the project and being my ally early on. And to my photographers: Shana

Sureck, Bill Bamberger, Bruce Antink, and Louis Shackleton for their beautiful portraits of each person I interviewed. Thanks to all of my transcribers and interns Isaac Price-Slade, Scott Groffman, Betsy Ericksen, Naomi Silverman, and Isabella Sanchez-Leo. Thanks to Karen Baker, Rebecca Busansky, Michael Cohen, Susan Gore, Heidi Haas, Mary Hickie, Esther Kohn, Alison Morse, Jerry O'Brien, and Dennis Powell for all their help and encouragement. Thanks to Peggy Gillespie for inspiration and generosity. Thanks to the great work of Tim Johnston and Sherrill Wayland of SAGE and the National Resource Center on LGBT Aging for helping me get the word out to elders who might be interested in becoming a part of the book and for giving it a place on their website. I would like to thank the staff at Skinner House Press for your enthusiasm: Mary Benard, Joni McDonald, Pierce Alquist, Kiana Nwaobia, Larisa Hohenboken, copy editor Shoshanna Green, text designer Jeff Miller, text designer and cover designer Kathryn Sky-Peck. I want to thank Enid and Norman Fleishman, Barbara Tabachnick, Ezra Fleishman, and Rosie Tabachnick, Paul and Carrie Fleishman, for unending support and love, endless rounds of ideas, and kindness. And I feel an enormous sense of gratitude toward my lover, Joan Tabachnick, who read every word, believed in me, and loved me through all the difficulties and promises and messiness of bringing this book into the world. I am grateful to her every day.

Index